Books by Joan Robinson

*

THE ACCUMULATION OF CAPITAL
AN ESSAY ON MARXIAN ECONOMICS
THE ECONOMICS OF IMPERFECT COMPETITION
INTRODUCTION TO THE THEORY OF EMPLOYMENT
ESSAYS ON THE THEORY OF ECONOMIC GROWTH

EXERCISES IN ECONOMIC ANALYSIS

BY

JOAN ROBINSON

LONDON
MACMILLAN & CO LTD
NEW YORK · ST MARTIN'S PRESS
1963

MACMILLAN AND COMPANY LIMITED
St Martin's Street London WC2
also Bombay Calcutta Madras Melbourne

THE MACMILLAN COMPANY OF CANADA LIMITED
Toronto

ST MARTIN'S PRESS INC
New York

PRINTED IN GREAT BRITAIN

PREFACE

THIS is a text book of a somewhat unusual kind. Instead of presenting the student with some propositions which he is expected to master and to believe I have tried to show him how propositions in economic theory are arrived at so that he can carry on for himself where the book leaves off. This cannot be done by trying to explain analytical method. Sermons on methodology are of no use to a beginner. The only way to learn it is to do it.

I should, however, like to draw attention to a few methodological rules that I have tried to observe (if I have failed, the reader must catch me out).

(1) We must take time seriously. To make a comparison between two situations, each with its own future and its own past, is not the same thing as to trace a movement from one to the other.

(2) A quantity has no meaning unless we can specify the units in which it is measured.

(3) Technical and physical relations, between man and nature, must be distinguished from social relations, between man and man. (There is an intermediate class, concerning the incentives of behaviour, where human nature itself is part of the technical situation.)

Chewed in solitude, the exercises will prove very dry. The best way to use them is as a basis for group discussion. Each student should work over an exercise and then compare his results with others and discuss their meaning and application.

Part One, Section I, is concerned with the basic technical relations of production and introduces the

famous *law of diminishing returns*. The family stands
for any group, say a nation, whose fate we are interested
in, taken as a whole, without respect to the distribution
of tasks and benefits within it.

In Section II, we introduce the concept of a *production
function* and discuss problems of investment planning.
The whole of Part One lays the foundation for a discussion of the problems of under-developed countries.

Part Two, Section I, is important in illustrating the
third methodological rule mentioned above. Section II
introduces capitalist development and leads up both to
theories of long-run growth and to Keynes' theory of
employment. (No exercises are offered on the last topic,
for which there are many introductory books available;
very little attention is paid to monetary problems and
none, in this context, to international trade.)

Part Three provides the basis for understanding a
large part of traditional economic theory, including the
classical theory of international trade. It leads up to a
discussion of problems of primary-producer countries.

Part Four is somewhat sketchy; the subject matter
does not lend itself readily to treatment at this level.
Its main purpose is to outline a theory of the firm in
which time is taken seriously. It leads up to a discussion
of price policy.

Part Five is set out somewhat differently from the
rest. The scheme of thought is based on Marshall's
theory of short- and long-period price in conditions of
perfect competition, and the diagramatic exercises are
not indicated, being available in many text books. At
the same time the reader is asked to imagine an ideal
economy and invited to compare his own conceptions
with mine.

I am indebted for criticisms and comment to a
number of colleagues, in particular Professor H. G.

Johnson, Professor J. E. Meade and Dr. A. K. Sen, and to the lecture class with whom I went over Parts One and Two.

JOAN ROBINSON

CAMBRIDGE
September 1959

CONTENTS

PART TWO:
ACCUMULATION AND DISTRIBUTION

PART THREE:
AN EXCHANGE ECONOMY

PART FOUR:
CAPITALIST INDUSTRY

PART FIVE:
RATIONAL PRICE SYSTEM

INTRODUCTION

ECONOMICS does not offer, like the well-developed
natural sciences, a body of knowledge which the lay
public can accept as established. Economic facts, for the
most part, are either so general as to be obvious (a man
must eat to live) or so particular as to be uninteresting
(Bank rate is declared on Thursdays). A generalisation
of the 'laws of economics' usually turns out to be so
guarded as to be circular, depending for its validity on
its own definitions, or so riddled with exceptions as to
be of little use as a guide to practical affairs.This
unsatisfactory state of the subject is due to the fact
that settled conclusions cannot emerge from argument
unless there is an agreed method of deciding who is
right. In the laboratory sciences a crucial experiment
can be set up to test a hypothesis and can be carried
out and repeated according to rules which scientists
accept as valid. When a hypothesis is proved wrong,
the scientist who put it up has to withdraw it with
what grace he may. The hypotheses which have so far
survived constitute the body of science. In economic
affairs it is impossible to carry out experiments under
properly controlled conditions. The economist has to
proceed by interpreting the events which happen to be
thrown up in the course of history, and there is no
generally accepted code of rules for interpreting history.
Economics therefore consists of a tangled mass of
imperfectly tested hypotheses—about how an economy
works, why one economy differs from another, what
consequences are to be expected from particular events

or particular policies, and so forth. This is in the nature of the case and it is vain to deplore it.

For better or worse, the subject does exist. In the course of its evolution certain methods of thought have been worked out which are found to be useful (provided that their limitations are understood) as well as amusing. It is in order to master these methods that the student embarks upon a course of exercises in economic analysis.

The principal method in use is commonly described as 'building a model'. The model consists in a highly simplified mental picture, exhibiting the behaviour of people in a social and physical environment, which eliminates what is inessential to the problem in hand so as to focus attention on what is essential.

The simplifying assumptions which economists habitually make, if taken literally, would often be fantastic or comical. There is no point in drawing consequences from an assumption that is made merely to abstract from complications inessential to the argument in hand. For instance, when for a particular question we, say, assume a homogeneous labour force, there is no point in trying to make out what life would be like if their age and sex had no effect upon human beings. It does not matter how drastic the assumptions are, provided that they can be relaxed without destroying the basis of the argument that has been erected on them.

It is impossible to write out in full all the assumptions that are made in setting up a particular model. The writer has to rely upon the reader to fill in a great deal from common experience. A crabbed reader, who refuses to play, can always pick holes in what an economist says. For instance, suppose the economist says: 'When more labour is applied to a given area of cultivable land the product increases.' The crabbed reader may comment: 'Nonsense. Crops depend mainly upon the weather, and usually a good crop has involved less work than a poor one.' Obviously the economist meant his proposition to be subject to the condition 'given the weather', and of the two it is the pert reader who has made a fool of himself.

On the other hand, the reader of goodwill often finds that he has not been given sufficient guidance as to what he is supposed to be assuming about the background in which the problem in hand is set. In particular, English economists, from Ricardo to Keynes, have been accustomed to assume as a tacitly accepted background the institutions and problems of the England each of his own day; when their works are studied in other climes and other periods by readers who import other assumptions, a great deal of confusion and argument at cross-purposes arises in consequence.

In setting out these exercises I have tried to get over this difficulty by indicating very broadly the type of economic system in which each problem is discussed, and relying upon the goodwill of the reader to make sense rather than nonsense of the argument whenever he finds it possible to do so.

ECONOMIC SYSTEMS

There are certain economic problems which every human society has to deal with in one way or another. There must be property (whether individual, collective or co-operative) in the right to use land, and in means of production (tools, machinery, seed corn) and means of consumption (clothes, houses, stocks in the larder). There must be some way of organising production, and some way of distributing the product. In societies which are at all complicated there has to be some kind of monetary system and some way of providing for the expenses of administration. The manner in which such problems are dealt with in each society, embodied in law, custom and accepted morality, constitute the framework within which its economic system operates.

Human societies have operated under a fantastic variety of different types of system, each with sub-types and cross-mixtures. For our present purposes we shall pick out three pure types, each highly simplified compared to any actually known. To illustrate some points we make use of a society of free peasants, where a family owns land, and organises production and consumption for its own purposes. For other problems we use a pure socialist economy (more pure than any that actually exists) in which all property is owned collectively and production and distribution are organised on a collective plan administered by some organ of the state. Finally, we consider a pure capitalist system, where property is owned by a relatively small group of families and work performed by the rest in return for wages. In the first and the last case we abstract altogether from the existence of an apparatus of government. We are chiefly interested in the capitalist economy and consider the other two mainly in order to throw light upon it by way of contrast.

ANALYTICAL METHOD

Most economic questions lead up to a discussion of what consequences may be expected to follow a certain event. We cannot isolate a particular causal element from its surrounding circumstances by a controlled experiment. For instance, suppose that we want to know the consequences of having a larger population in a given space. We cannot find two identical countries and make the population change in one while it is held constant in another. Nor can we get very far by direct observation. We can compare two countries with different densities of population at a given moment, but they are different in many other respects besides. Or we can compare the same country at different dates, before and after the population has changed, but much else has happened meanwhile. Moreover, the internal constitution of the population to-day (in particular, its age composition) is different according as it is in course of growing, declining or remaining stationary.

We have to proceed by breaking the question up into parts, and after discussing each separately reassemble the pieces as best we may.

First, compare two economies which are alike in all relevant respects except the one which we wish to isolate (for the population question we should compare two economies with different numbers of the same age composition, and also compare two economies with the same numbers or the same labour force but different age compositions). Each has its own past and its own expectations about its own future. They need not be in stationary conditions provided that any change that has been taking place or is expected is smooth and regular so that we know where we are with it.

Next consider a single economy, following a regular predictable path, and consider how its subsequent course is altered by an event happening at a particular moment (say, a burst of immigration or a sudden fall in the birth rate).

Then consider an economy which is not following a smooth path, but is caught for examination, so to speak, at a particular moment in a more or less turbulent history. We have to try to work out what future development is inherent in the situation as it exists to-day (say, what change in numbers over the fore-seeable future is entailed by an abnormal age composition to-day).

Finally, we have to try to see what effect upon this in any case turbulent path would be introduced by a particular event.

This is all extremely confusing and even the best practitioners are liable to go astray. The first stage in a training in analysis is to learn to recognise what question is being discussed. The main purpose of these exercises is no more than to sort out questions.

PART ONE

PRODUCTION AND ACCUMULATION

THE exercises contained in Parts One and Two are all concerned with output as a whole, not with the pattern of output of various goods or with relative prices. We therefore want to make one sweeping assumption that will clear out of the way all considerations concerned with particular commodities. There is no need to strain the imagination to picture a "one-commodity world" in which people dress in corn as well as eat it, or eat cloth as well as wear it. We can postulate that final consumers buy units of a composite commodity always made up in the same way. Various items in the "basket" of goods may be produced separately and there may be separate stages of production and different items of equipment for any one of them. We do not want to be tied up with more simplifying assumptions than are strictly necessary. All we need is to be able to talk about the flow of output of consumer goods, their price level, the labour required to produce them, etc., without having to stop to argue about the difference made to these various quantities by differences in the composition of output. We shall find a number of questions which are quite complicated to discuss even when they have been so very drastically simplified.

I. THE FAMILY ECONOMY

OUR first concern is certain relations between land, labour and production which are the basis of all economic systems. In order to see them in their simplest form we deploy them in the setting of the simplest kind of economic system.

Our model economy consists of a single family, settled on a particular stretch of land, producing entirely for its own consumption. The internal organisation of the family (in particular, the manner in which work is allotted to various members and the means of consumption distributed) follows rules that are perfectly acceptable to all, so that there are no conflicts of interest within the family and we can treat it as an entity which can be said to work, consume, accumulate property, and so forth, as though it were an individual human being, but an immortal one. We assume that it is subject to economic motives in the sense that there are material goods of which it always prefers more to less, provided, at least, that they can be got without more effort; and that it prefers less to greater effort, provided, at least, that it yields no less goods.

There are some economies of scale even in the simplest productive techniques—two men can fell a tree in less than half the time that one man would take. Except when notice is given to the contrary, we eliminate this phenomenon by postulating that the family is large enough to enjoy the economies appropriate to the techniques that they are using.

I. DIMINISHING RETURNS

First, suppose that our family is situated in an empty fertile plain and that it can use as much land as it pleases. Up to a certain point, the more land the more product, but this obviously cannot be true indefinitely. Assuming all the land alike, all workers equally industrious and equally capable, and uniform techniques in use, there is one degree of intensity of cultivation, or ratio of land to labour, which yields the highest return per man-year of work. When this ratio is established the *marginal product of land*, from the point of view of the family, is equal to zero in the sense that if a slightly larger area were cultivated, with the amount of work that the family is able and willing to do, the product would be no greater than with a slightly smaller area. (If they cultivated an appreciably larger area the product would actually be less. More land might be sown, but part of the old harvest lost through lack of hands to get it in.) The marginal product of labour is equal to its average product at the optimum land-labour ratio, for there would be no point in cultivating some land more intensively and getting an additional product less than might be obtained by deploying the labour on more space. (We will discuss the problem of breaking in new land later—here we are simply comparing the productivities of different degrees of intensity of cultivation already established.)

Now compare families which are different in size though alike in every other respect (including age composition), assuming that the working members of a family always have the same equipment. (The problems of change in size of a family will be discussed in a moment—here we are comparing different hypothetical sizes, each as it would be if it were already in being.)

Since land is freely available, the area cultivated by a family is proportionate to its labour force, and the size of the family does not affect output per man-year of work or output per acre. Output per man-year is at the maximum compatible with the amount of work that the family is able and willing to provide.

When land is boundless the family can decide the area they will cultivate on economic principles, but they do not adjust the numbers in the family on economic principles. Anyone who gets himself born shares the family work and the family product. When space is restricted the land-labour ratio is determined by the size of the family. Let us now compare families of various sizes all living in exactly similar regions, with the same space available to each.

A family whose labour exceeds the amount that can enjoy the optimum land-labour ratio has less than the maximum possible output per head, for more work on the same soil yields a less than proportional increase in output. Output per head falls progressively as the land-labour ratio falls. The *marginal product of labour*, that is the additional annual output due to an additional man-year of labour in the given space, is less than the average output per man-year.

There is a certain maximum total output that can be extracted from the soil with the known techniques. The size of the family may then be such that, with the land they happen to have, the marginal product of labour is zero, in the sense that members of the family have time on their hands when there is nothing that they can do, with the techniques which they know, to increase output. The marginal product of labour may even be negative (bodies get in each other's way, or spells of idleness demoralise the workers).

When the land-labour ratio is below the optimum, conditions of *diminishing returns* are said to prevail. The word "diminishing" suggests a process going on through time, but we are so far only concerned with comparisons of hypothetical states, and time and motion do not come into the argument.

Figure 1(a)

These relationships can be set out in a diagram. Take output per man-year on the vertical or y axis and labour working in the given space on the horizontal or x axis, and trace the relationship between the average and marginal output per unit of labour and the quantity of labour. Up to the point where the optimum is passed, the two curves coincide and are horizontal. As we move further to the right (with rising values of x) the land-labour ratio falls below the optimum, average output per man-year begins to fall, and therefore the marginal output lies below the average. When total output is at the maximum possible, marginal output is zero. For any point, P, on the average curve, show the rectangle which represents total output.

Figure 1(b)

The same relationships can be shown in another way. With the same x axis as before, take total annual output on the y axis. The curve is at first a straight line rising to the right (north-eastward) from the origin, O. Its slope represents average output per unit of labour. At the quantity of labour where the land-labour ratio falls below the optimum the curve becomes convex (the slope grows progressively less steep as the quantity of labour increases). At the point of maximum possible total output the curve becomes horizontal (parallel to the x axis).

2. EXTENSIVE AND INTENSIVE MARGINS

We must now consider different qualities of the soil—for instance, we may imagine that our family lives in a bowl of land. At larger and larger sizes the family works higher and higher up the hillside, where return per unit of work grows progressively less. Now there is no stretch of constant returns; diminishing returns are shown for each increase in work done. A larger amount of product can be extracted by more work in two ways—by increasing the intensity of cultivation in a given area or by extending the area. For each amount of work there is one best way of distributing the labour over the land. The condition of an optimum distribution of labour over the space means that nothing is to be gained either by extending the area cultivated, taking some of the given labour force off the better land to do so, or by retracting the area and increasing the intensity of cultivation on what remains. That is to say, at the optimum, the marginal product of labour is equal on each portion of the land, and is equal to the total product of a unit of labour on the marginal land.

Figure 2

To illustrate, draw a number of diagrams like Figure 1(a), each for a particular area of land, the product curve leaving the y axis at different points in each. It can immediately be seen that, the total quantity of labour being given, the total product can be increased so long as it is possible to transfer labour from a point of lower to a point of higher marginal product, so that total product is maximised when the marginal product is the same all over the area being cultivated. This is known as the equalisation of productivity on the *intensive* and the *extensive* margin. The principle here shown is useful in many contexts in economic analysis.

3. GROWTH AND INVESTMENT

Let us now return to the boundless plain and consider the process of growth of our family. We now assume that land has to be cleared before it can be used. In order to have a base to mark off from, let us compare a stationary with a growing family. The age composition of a growing family is different from that of a stationary one, and this is likely to affect their pattern of consumption, but we are not going into that aspect of the matter here. Nor do we consider growth starting at a particular moment, out of a stationary past (this involves some complications that will be discussed later), but assume that the same state of affairs has continued for some time, and that each family is adjusted to its own situation.

When numbers are stationary, to preserve for coming generations the same level of consumption that has been enjoyed in the past, it is only necessary to keep the area cultivated and the stock of equipment constant. When each generation is going to be larger than the last, to preserve a constant level of consumption per head requires that the stock of means of production should grow as fast as the labour force. Every year new land has to be broken in, ploughs provided, more animals reared and so forth. Part of present work is then not for present consumption but *investment* to provide means of production in the future.

There are various ways in which means of production can be accumulated. The working members of the family may put in more time in clearing land, etc., while producing and consuming the same amount of current output per head as in a stationary population and maintaining the pre-existing stock of equipment. But it may be that harder work requires more consumption (the easy-going need less calories) or it may be that family tradition requires that whoever works more receives more from current product. Then they have also to be working harder to provide for current consumption (and perhaps cultivating more land) in order to support the extra work on investment.

It may, however, be physically impossible to produce enough both to maintain consumption at the level enjoyed by a stationary population and to provide for the future. Then they must be doing less work for current consumption, and the burden of *abstinence* (the lower consumption made necessary by the investment) has to be distributed over the family in one way or another. If the consumption of working members cannot be cut, others must be stinted, or the provision of equipment for the new generation will fall below standard, and production per head will gradually decline as time goes by.

It is to be observed that the burden which growth imposes upon the family is nothing whatever to do with diminishing returns from land, for we are assuming land is uniform and freely available. If our growing family were in a bowl instead of on a plain, successive generations would be suffering from the effects of ever diminishing returns, as well as each generation having to struggle with the duty to provide for its successors.

4. SHRINKING POPULATION

The process of reducing the size of the family is not symmetrical with the process of growth (even apart from the question of age-composition which we are not discussing here). When we set out the comparative productivity of families of different sizes we can run our eye up or down the curve as we please, but time imposes a strict rule of one-way traffic. A smaller generation which inherits ready-broken-in land and ready-made equipment from a larger generation is freed not only from the need to invest in increasing stocks, but also (if the decline in numbers is large relatively to the rate at which equipment wears out) from the need to maintain the existing stock (redundant ploughs can be kept in store and worn out one after another). In short, it can enjoy a higher ratio of consumption to work than could a stationary population of the same size. On the other hand, some of the inherited equipment (including drainage, irrigation works, etc.) may be inappropriate to its needs, or it may even be a nuisance so that it costs some investment to clear it away; and there is a danger that, living too long with ready-made equipment, the family may lose the skill and knowledge of its ancestors and be unable to replace equipment when the stock has finally been exhausted.

5. 'OPTIMUM POPULATION'

Quite apart from loss of skill, the mere fact of continually reducing the total labour force and the over-all flow of production must sooner or later carry the family below the point at which economies of scale begin to be lost.

The opposing tendencies of gain from raising the land-labour ratio and loss from forgoing economies of scale leads to the notion of an *optimum size of population*, at which average output per head is a maximum, but this idea belongs to the realm of comparisons of economies of different sizes, each already in being; the asymmetry between growth and decline makes it very hazy when applied to changes in size, and it becomes still more so when we introduce technical progress, which is at present being kept out of our model.

6. ACCUMULATION

Even if the family is stationary in numbers it may carry out investment in order to enhance productivity in the future. Starting with any given stock of means of production, they cannot get very far by merely increasing the stock of the same type, for the marginal product of land, of ploughs, of fertilisers, etc., falls off sharply as the amount used of each increases with a given labour force. The technical nature of equipment will have to be changed as the stock is increased. This may be done partly merely by *waiting*, that is postponing consumption and allowing natural processes to ripen, as when the stock of timber is increased by refraining from felling part-grown trees; and it may be done partly by direct abstinence, as when seed-corn is set aside for sowing instead of being eaten. But in general investment consists of doing work to build equipment which will last a long time, to improve personal efficiency by training, or to start on a process of production (say, ploughing and sowing additional land) which will more than make good the current rate of consumption. Some elements of abstinence and of waiting are bound up with this work—abstinence in so far as it means that the ratio of current consumption to current work is less than it would be if investment were not going on, and waiting since time must go by before the benefit of it can be enjoyed.

Very often there are alternative possible ways of combining labour and waiting, so that for a given amount of current work there is a choice between a smaller return in the near future and a larger return in the more distant future.

Investment to equip more workers operating at the pre-established land-labour ratio, with the pre-existing type of equipment and in the already established time-pattern of production, is described as *widening*, and the investment such as we have just been discussing, which increases the future productivity of a given labour force within a given framework of technical knowledge, is described as *deepening*. An increase in the land-labour ratio which comes about through breaking in new land may be regarded as a form of deepening, but it is better to use other terms for the types of increase in the quantity per head of land and durable equipment that come about through a shrinkage of population and through a decline of activity.

7. 'THE MARGINAL PRODUCT OF CAPITAL'

When we compared families employing different ratios of land to labour we assumed that each worker had the same equipment and followed the same time pattern of production. The 'factors of production' were land already broken-in and labour-plus-means-of-production. It would be convenient if we could lump all equipment and work in progress together as a third 'factor of production' and separate its marginal product from that of labour, but this involves a number of puzzles of definition and measurement. We can compare the productivity of a given labour force equipped in one way or another (to see what difference equipment makes) but the alternative products will generally be spread over the future in different time-patterns and require different amounts of labour to produce them. If we try to express each as a perpetual even flow, by assuming that a stock of equipment once built up is permanently maintained, debiting its maintenance cost against its output, we have to compare different replacements falling due at different dates, so that the cost of replacement is by no means a straightforward calculation. Thus we cannot compare the values of two schemes of investment in terms of their future productivity in any simple way. Nor can we compare their costs in terms of efforts and sacrifices in a simple way. Waiting, abstinence, the performance of work and the use of pre-existing equipment and materials have gone into past investment in different mixtures; and there is no simple way of evaluating them.

There are even greater difficulties in saying what we mean by the marginal product of labour separately from means of production. We can define the short-period marginal product of labour with a given physical stock of equipment (see below §18(i)) but in general with a different quantity of labour it is appropriate to use equipment of a different kind, and if we said that the 'same amount' of equipment is assumed to be fitted to different quantities of labour in appropriate forms, we should be very much puzzled to know what the 'same amount' is supposed to mean.

However, these are just puzzles—problems not about what is but about what we should call it—and they need not worry us, so long as we are careful always to mean no less than we say and to say no more than we mean.

8. STATIONARY STATES

Before discussing in more detail a process of accumulation with a constant labour force it is necessary to be clear what we mean by stationary conditions.

First of all, stationary conditions require the size and the age and sex composition of the family to be constant through time; tastes, habits, skill, knowledge and general attitudes of mind in all relevant respects to be unchanging; and, of course, all relevant natural conditions to be constant. But this is not enough to specify stationariness. There must also be a steady rate of output and of consumption. This entails that there is no accumulation of means of production going on (whether by work or prolonging of gestation periods) while there must be continuous replacement to keep the existing stock of equipment in being.

We can distinguish three attitudes that may account for this state of affairs. The first is that the family does not accumulate simply because it does not occur to them to do so; they conduct their affairs on a basis of tradition. They go on with what they have. At the same time they feel that it would be wrong or undesirable to allow the rate of output to fall. Each generation keeps their stock of means of production of each type up to the level that it was when they inherited it. The total stock in existence is just an historical accident.

At the other extreme, the family may be willing and able to accumulate indefinitely, but they have reached the stage where no increase in the stock of equipment or lengthening of gestation periods would add anything to the flow of output. They have reached the stage of saturation of investment possibilities or *economic bliss*. A part of their labour force is still engaged in producing equipment, for the stock has to be kept intact by replacements of what wears out. If through negligence or accident the stock of equipment fell, the urge to accumulate would re-assert itself and the economy would be carried back to bliss.

An intermediate case is one in which the family can see quite clearly that investment would add to their productive capacity but it does not seem to them worth the effort and abstinence that it involves, either because their level of consumption is low, relatively to their ideas of what is comfortable, and work already hard, so that the effort would be very great (though they are able to maintain what they have); or because they are already so comfortable that to gain a somewhat higher standard of future consumption does not seem worth even a small effort (though it is worth an effort to avoid a cut). In these cases the stock of means of production in existence depends on the psychology and traditions of the family concerned, as well as upon the technical conditions with which they are faced.

9. DEEPENING INVESTMENT

To discuss accumulation it is obviously of no use to start off from an economy which is already in bliss, or as near to it as it is able or as it is willing to get. As our basis of comparison, we take the family of Esses who are in a stationary state of the first kind. They happen to be producing and consuming at a certain level and carry on from year to year always doing what they have always done. The Gees, on the other hand, are (and long have been) continually carrying out deepening investment. The two families are alike in every other relevant respect (including the land available to each) and both are constant in size. We compare them at a base date when each family is doing the same amount of work per annum, and when the Gees have just reached the 'depth' of equipment and work in progress that the Esses have always enjoyed.

The latter proviso involves a puzzle of definition, for the two economies are producing outputs of different composition—the Gees' output being partly additional means of production while the Esses are only replacing current consumption. If it is possible to draw a hard and fast line between replacements and additions, then we can say that our proviso means that the work that is providing for current consumption is carried on in Geeland with just the same means of production, just the same techniques and in the same time pattern, as in Esseland. If such a sharp separation is not possible because the activities devoted to investment modify those devoted to providing for consumption, then we have to fall back on common sense and give a rough and ready definition of what we propose to mean by the 'same depth'.

The level of consumption of the Gees is less than that of the Esses, for the work being done is the same and on any reasonable definition is equally productive, while for the Gees some of it is directed to investment and for the Esses all is directed to maintaining the level of consumption. As time goes by and investment bears fruit, output per man-year of work increases for the Gees while it remains constant for the Esses.

Figure 3

To illustrate, set up a diagram with time on the x axis, the origin, O, being the base date for our story. Mark it with an arrow pointing to the right to indicate one-way traffic. On the y axis we can measure consumption per annum, for we have boldly assumed that consumption can be measured in homogeneous units ('baskets' of goods). It would be more convenient to measure output (including additions to stocks of equipment, etc.) but we cannot do so because it is not homogeneous. The distance OG on the y axis represents the consumption of the Gee family at the base date. OS (greater than OG) is the consumption of the Esses. The S line, perpendicular to the y axis at S, exhibits the constancy through time of the Esses' consumption.

OB (*B* lying on the *y* axis above *S*) represents the level of consumption at bliss, that is, the highest level of consumption that can be continuously maintained given the natural conditions, the technical conditions and tastes, knowledge, and all relevent human characteristics (which are the same for both families). The *B* line is parallel to the *S* line, for we are assuming (quite arbitrarily, of course) that all this remains constant through time.

The discussion of what happens to the Gees' output and consumption can be illustrated as we go along.

How should we draw the line representing the behaviour of the Gees' consumption through time? There is a wide range of possibilities, depending upon natural and technical considerations, and on the economic behaviour of the family.

To separate the two sets of influences we will first assume that the technical conditions are very simple. We will postulate that the *marginal productivity of investment* is constant in the sense that, over the relevant range, a given amount of work done in adding to the stock of means of production procures a given increment in productivity for the future. For instance, we may imagine that the only kind of investment that remains to be done is in improving the drainage of the land. The workers are already supplied with an adequate stock of perfectly durable tools, and a man-year of work improves a definite area of land in such a way as permanently to increase its yield without any need for extra work in cultivating it. When our story begins there is a large area of land awaiting improvement.

Now, if a certain amount of work is allotted to drainage each year (other activities remaining the same), and the extra produce is consumed as it becomes available, then output and consumption both increase at a regular rate of so much per annum, and the G curve, representing the consumption of the Gees, is a straight line rising to the right, with a slope which indicates the increase in the rate of output occurring per unit of time. After a certain time, depending upon the initial gap and the slope of the G curve, it crosses the S line (showing the date at which consumption of the Gees begins to rise above that of the Esses), and after a further time the G curve hits the B line and investment abruptly comes to an end.

There is no need, however, for this path to be followed. In one set of technical conditions a wide range of alternative programmes of investment are open to choose from. One possibility is that, as consumption increases, the family becomes willing and able to do more work, so that the area of land drained each year increases. This is represented by drawing the curve concave upwards, the slope becoming steeper as it rises, so that the level of consumption is rushing all the faster towards bliss. On the other hand, they may slacken off as wealth increases, so that the curve is convex and approaches bliss asymptotically, without ever reaching it. More complicated shapes are possible. Output and consumption may be kept constant for a time and then increased sharply (say, labour is saved on harvesting in order to speed up the improvement of a larger area). Or output may be kept up but consumption restrained so as to build up liquid stocks. In each respect the policy of the family may pass through various phases as its productive capacity gradually changes, so that the curve pursues a serpentine course.

These variations depend upon the reaction of the family to simple technical conditions. Technical conditions may also be very various. In our example of drainage, output per acre and output per unit of labour were increased equally. This is a fluke case. In general, investment may have a bias either in the direction of reducing land per unit of output more than labour (say, irrigation) or in the direction of reducing labour more than land (better implements). It may even be necessary actually to reduce output per head in order to benefit from a new means of increasing output per acre or *vice versa*. The choice of the family as to which kind of investment to go in for is partly constrained by technical conditions and partly influenced by economic motivations. (For instance, if they are willing to work but have limited land, labour-saving land-using investments are of no use to them.)

The assumption of constant returns to investment was also quite arbitrary. By and large, speaking with deliberate vagueness (for precision in this context is highly artificial) we should expect returns in terms of increased productivity to fall off as successive rounds of investment succeed each other, for the most rewarding investments will be chosen first, so that the greater the investment that has already been done, the greater the effort (in terms of work, waiting and abstinence) required to achieve a given increment of productivity. Diminishing returns in general tend to give convexity to the G curve—it tends to flatten out as it rises towards bliss. But this is not an invariable rule and the curve may be full of twists and jerks. For one thing, the gestation period of different investments is very different, so that there may be an occasional sudden spurt of output (and so of consumption) when a large scheme yields its first fruit. Sometimes there may be an actual decline of consumption because a particular scheme must be carried out quickly or not at all and hands have to be called off current output to complete it. (The need to reduce consumption, however, does not arise in so far as liquid stocks have been amassed in advance.) Again, a particularly rewarding investment may become possible only after a considerable 'depth' has already been reached, so that better investments are made after worse ones. In short, we must put a few wobbles into the G curve in order to remind ourselves that the process of accumulation going on through time, with given technical possibilities, is under no obligation to follow any simple formula.

10. ACCUMULATION AND DIMINISHING RETURNS

We may now return for a moment to the case of increasing population in a limited space. When equipment per worker is kept constant, as we assumed before, output per head falls as the ratio of labour to land rises. Even to keep up the level of equipment per man, as we saw, involves a burden on the family, and in these conditions it is hard for them to increase equipment per head, but they may succeed in doing so. With a sufficient effort of accumulation and in propitious technical conditions, it may be possible to fend off a falling level of output per head, or even to increase it over a certain range, by improving equipment per head to make up for dwindling land per head. It is important to notice that in such a case investments which merely save labour are much less useful than those which increase output per acre.

11. ACCELERATING ACCUMULATION

We assumed that the Gees were already engaged in a process of deepening when we first observed them. Now let us investigate a *rise* in the rate of accumulation. Suppose that the Esses, who have long been in a stationary state, suddenly rouse themselves and decide to embark on a programme of investment.

If they are already fully extended the only way to start investment is to switch some resources from providing for consumption. Generally speaking, the bigger the cut in consumption, the faster the rate of accumulation, but it is to be observed that if they go down to what was the Gees' level of consumption at the base date they will not be able to achieve the Gees' rate of growth immediately; they can release labour by cutting consumption, but the labour is not yet equipped and trained for its new activities, and the Esses will have to go further back, so to speak, into the Gees' past before it can overtake their present.

The situation is different if the Esses are able to do more work and have some sufficiently versatile tools. Then they need not cut consumption, but can devote extra work to investment. As output per head of consumption goods gradually rises (as new means of production come into use) they may still keep consumption constant, drafting the labour released over to investment and working up their rate of accumulation as rapidly as they can without an actual cut in consumption; or they may begin immediately to have some increase in consumption (or some relaxation of their first burst of extra work) and consequently a slower rate of rise over the future.

A similar exercise can be worked out for the case (which we neglected above) of an increase in the rate of growth of population.

As we have already seen in the story of the Gees, a combination of various technical conditions with various types of economic behaviour can lead to pretty well any pattern of development and the reader can elaborate, combine and vary the exercises according to his own fancy.

12. PROPER BEHAVIOUR

Is there any standard for the proper rate of accumulation? I do not think that there is. There is no way of evaluating present work against future consumption, or a permanent flow of future consumption against a once-for-all sacrifice in the present. We may say that if consumption per head is in any case rising through time, so that future generations are going to be more comfortable, we should reckon that it is more onerous to forgo consumption now than it will be later, but just what allowance to make for this consideration cannot be laid down in any generally acceptable rule.

The rate of accumulation that a family undertakes is an effect of its general character, expressing its foresight, self-discipline, sense of duty to the future, and appetite for economic improvement, playing against its love of leisure, self-indulgence or contempt for worldly goods.

If some bright spark amongst them sets up as an economist, he cannot tell the rest of the family what they ought to do. He may, however, influence their attitudes by making them conscious of what they are doing and helping them to be aware of what benefits would follow from what efforts. At the same time he may distort their natural good sense by overweighting the measurable aspects of the problem (which he likes talking about) at the expense of imponderables that are actually more important. But the economic effects of economics is too subtle a subject to take up in these exercises.

II. A SOCIALIST ECONOMY

THE family in our first model lives in a state of innocence, without internal conflicts. All questions concerning production and distribution are settled directly, in concrete terms, on the merits of each case (according to the views of what is right and fair prevalent in the family). There is no need for a valuation of goods or services or for payments between individuals, for all economic behaviour is governed by accepted duties and admitted rights.

We now move on to discuss a larger society which cannot be run purely on morality. We may call it a nation or a country, but it is the only one. It has no problems of defence and no opportunities for external trade. Like the isolated family, it is a *closed system*.

All means of production are owned by the nation collectively and are organised in factories, farms, shops, etc., and administered on an integrated plan. (There is no peasant or co-operative sector such as exists in actual socialist countries to-day.)

Stocks of equipment in existence are a long way from bliss but there will be no technical progress in the sense of new discoveries and inventions, for the best possible methods of production are already foreknown. Much 'deeper' productive methods are available than it has yet been possible to install.

Some services (say, medical treatment) are provided to the citizen as required, and some (say, education, law and order and general administration) are provided willy-nilly. Other means of consumption (which we still assume to be used in definite 'basketfuls') are sold through the shops for money tokens.

The distribution of purchasing power over these *commodities* (that is, consumer goods which are sold for money) is made according to a rigorous application of the rule 'to each according to his work', that is to say, the only way of acquiring money tokens is by working for wages, under the direction of the national administrators, who are themselves working for wages.

We are in any case doing exercises on a 'one-commodity world' and we may as well maintain the utmost simplicity by assuming also that all workers alike, and all receiving a standard rate of pay for a standard week's work.

13. PRICES AND WAGES

The first question which we will take up is the determination of the real wage rate in terms of commodities—that is the purchasing power over commodities of the money paid per man-week of work. The money-wage rate is quite arbitrary—words and numbers written on paper. Taking a view, in the light of technical possibilities, of current and future needs (which will be discussed later) the authorities have allocated workers to providing free services; to replacing current consumption of commodities (or rather current sales, for no one asks at what rate goods are consumed, in the privacy of the household, after they have been bought) and replacing means of production used up in producing them; to productive investment, that is, to increasing the stock of equipment of all kinds and to starting processes which will increase the future rate of output (building up work in progress); and to social investment in housing and amenities. The workers taken as a whole receive a certain total of money wages per week. The available commodities have to be shared amongst the workers, and to make the system run smoothly, without gluts or shortages, the level of prices must be set so that the value of current output just matches the volume of money expenditure. Prices have nothing to do with the real scarcity of goods in relation to needs. If by mistake prices were set too high so that there was not enough wage-income to buy current output, goods would pile up in the shops and there would be an appearance of superfluity. If they are set too low, latecomers to the queues find nothing to spend their money on.

The correct setting of prices is not a simple matter. It would not do to set a price that 'clears the market', for the goods in the shops to-day are a stock representing many weeks' output, and if they were all sold this week there would be a violent downward bump in supply next week. The art is to set prices so that the quantities that purchasers want to buy at those prices are related to current output in such a way as to keep stocks at the appropriate level, increasing somewhat if the rate of output and sales are rising as time goes by. (These matters are further discussed in Part Five.)

Assuming that this art has been mastered so that prices are always correctly set, we can work out the relation between prices and money wages. This is most easily done by means of a numerical example. Let us call the wage per man-week one pound, and the output per man-week of those producing goods for sale, one basket. Now suppose that, say, 60 per cent. of the labour force is engaged in this sector and the other 40 per cent. on non-saleable output. Then, when all money incomes are currently spent, the price of a basket is £1⅔ and the real wage per man-week is ·6 of a basket. The surplus of the value of output over the wages bill for saleable goods is equal to the wages bill for non-saleable goods, and the proceeds of the sales provide the funds required to pay the wages. 60 men

in the consumption sector produce goods to be sold for
£100 (the wage-income of 100 men) of which they buy
£60 worth themselves, leaving enough to meet £40 of
demand from others. At the same time, the profit
made on the sale of their product (£100−60) provides
the authorities with funds to pay the producers of
non-saleable output.

For those who feel happier in algebra:—

w = money wage per man-week

b = output per man-week in the consumption
     goods sector

p = price of basket

L_c = number of workers engaged in the con-
     sumption goods sector

L = total number of workers

Then $p = \dfrac{wL}{bL_c}$

$$\frac{w}{p} = \frac{bL_c}{L}$$

$$w(L - L_c) = (pb - w)L_c$$

All this expresses the assumptions that prices are
correctly set so as to absorb current money demand
and that all wages are currently spent. It is simply an
automatic result of the way the market works when it
fulfils these two conditions.

14. PERSONAL SAVING

Now remove the assumption that all money income is
spent. If the citizens save part of their receipts, so that
the flow of money expenditure is less than the wages
bill, prices are lower than in the first case, and consequently the real wage rate higher. Those who spend
get more for their money (eating up what the savers
abstain from buying) while the abstinence of the

savers (the difference between their real wage and their real purchases) is less than in proportion to their saving (the difference between their money income and money outlay).

The consumption of the public as a whole is unaffected by individual saving, for the total flow of production and sales of commodities was fixed in the general economic plan, independently of their behaviour. If all individuals saved the same proportion of their money incomes, no one's consumption would be affected at all; prices would be appropriately lower.

Contrariwise, if the citizens, drawing upon a stock of purchasing power built up by saving in the past, spend more than the wages bill, prices have to be higher, and the dis-savers suck away goods from the others. If all dis-save equally, again no one's consumption in fact alters.

It is a simple exercise to assume that a certain proportion of the workers save a certain proportion of their wages and to see the effect upon their own consumption and on that of the others. It is also interesting to work out the effect of erratic changes in the rate of expenditure, allowing the first impact to fall on stocks and working through to prices.

15. THE QUANTITY OF MONEY

The circulating medium is created by the authorities printing notes and using them to pay wages. If the complete circuit which a note makes, from the hand of a worker who receives it one pay-day back *via* a shop to the point where it is just about to be paid out to a worker again, takes, on the average, say, *n* weeks, then, in the case where private saving is unknown, the total stock of money in existence to-day is equal to the wages bill of the past *n* weeks.

Figure 4

This can be illustrated as follows. Take the horizontal distance OT to represent n weeks. The vertical TN is the money value of the wage bill that has just been paid out to-day and OM is that which was paid out OT weeks ago. MN is joined by a line whose height above OT represents the wage bill at each intermediate date.

If the wage bill has been constant, so that $TN = OM$, the quantity of money is represented by the rectangle $OM.OT$. If it has, say, been rising by a regular increment each week (for instance, with growing employment) MN is a straight line and the quantity of money is shown by $OM.OT$ plus the triangle whose base is OT and height $TN - OM$. More complicated cases are shown in correspondingly more variegated shapes.

If private saving is going on, there is a leakage of notes out of circulation into hoards. This is continuously made good by more printing, so that the quantity in active circulation is unaffected.

The holding of notes is a kind of interest-free loan to the nation, but the authorities may not like citizens to hold large hoards of notes for fear of the upsetting affect of an unforeseen burst of dis-saving. They may prefer to offer the public some kind of certificates which are rather tiresome to cash (so as to discourage impulsive spending) and which could be blocked in a crisis. In so far as current wages are used to buy certificates there is no scope for increasing the quantity of money to provide for hoards, and in so far as old hoards are turned out to buy certificates, notes are cancelled.

All this is a complication of little immediate relevance and for the moment we will assume that there is not, and never has been, any private saving or dis-saving,

and that no savings certificates or hoards of notes
exist in our model socialist economy. The stock of
notes in circulation then adjusts itself automatically
to requirements, and we need not bother any more
about it.

16. ABSORBING THE RESERVE OF LABOUR

We must now consider the investment programme
of the socialist economy. The question appears in two
different aspects according to whether or not we start
off in a state of full employment. In the family economy
all the work and all the product were shared round.
There may have been unwanted idleness, in the
sense that if the family had had, say, more land they
would have been pleased to do more work, but the
distinctions between unemployment, leisure and idleness were not at all sharp.

In the socialist economy a man is said to be employed
when he is working in the regular organised economy
and receiving money wages. We first consider a situation
in which the authorities have not yet been able to
organise work for all the potential labour force. There
are a mass of people living somehow or other outside
the organised system in very unsatisfactory conditions.
One reason why they cannot be put to work at once is
that the equipment in existence is all being used to the
hilt and there is no place for them to work. But even
if they could do something useful with their bare hands
there is still the problem of providing them with real
wages. To keep the stark lines of the argument clear
we will postulate that their present level of production
and consumption is so wretched as to be practically
nil, although they are busy all day just keeping alive.
If they were given jobs and paid wages, their expenditure
would suck up part of the output of commodities being

produced by organised industry and reduce the consumption of those already in regular employment.

This matter must be looked into with some care, and we are obliged to make even more drastic simplifications than hitherto to get the exercise on to its feet.

We suppose, at the first stage of the analysis, that there is just one kind of equipment, let us call it a 'plough', required for producing commodities, let us call them 'corn'. Ploughs can be built from freely available materials, so that, in effect they are made by labour alone. Some men are already using ploughs to produce corn in the organised economy. Their output per head is rigidly fixed by technical conditions. They consume less corn than they produce. The surplus is available to feed workers producing non-saleable output. To concentrate the problem, let us suppose that investment is the only kind of activity apart from the production of corn. The surplus, therefore, employs workers who are producing additional ploughs. As the stock of ploughs increases, more men are called in from the surrounding limbo of non-employment; they are set to work with the ploughs and begin to produce at the same rate as those already employed, thus providing not only a much better level of comsumption for themselves but also a surplus to support more plough makers. (To eliminate the complication of the build-up of work in progress we will suppose the gestation period of corn to be very short). Thus, granted an initial surplus of corn to support ploughmakers, the originally non-employed population can be gradually absorbed into the organised economy.

Suppose that the real wage per man-year is two-thirds of the corn that a man with a plough produces in a year, while four men in a year can build the plough that one will use. Then eight men ploughing can support four men who build a plough and make it possible to employ one more worker on ploughing next year. Eight teams of twelve working in these proportions for a year can set up another team of twelve (eight to plough and four to build a plough) who will provide for one more man ploughing the year after, and so on. Employment of men equipped with ploughs, and therefore total output, is increasing at the rate of $\frac{1}{8}$ per annum cumulatively.

In general:—

b = output of corn per man-plough-year

w = corn wage per man-year

k = number of men required to build in a year a plough to be used by one man

L_c = labour engaged in producing corn

L_i = labour engaged in producing additional ploughs

$$L = L_c + L_i$$

Then $L_i = \left(\dfrac{b}{w} - 1 \right) L_c$

$$L = \frac{b}{w} L_c$$

The rate of growth of employment is L_i/kL_c which is equal to $\dfrac{1}{k} \left(\dfrac{b}{w} - 1 \right)$

In all this the important thing to notice is that, other things equal, the rate of growth of employment is greater the lower is the real wage rate (provided that it is not so low as to impair efficiency) and that if the rate of growth of the output of ploughs (and so of employment) were allowed to slacken, the real wage rate would rise.

This creates a grim conflict of interest, between those already employed and the others, which the authorities must settle as best they may.

17. A CHOICE OF TECHNIQUE WITH
A RESERVE OF LABOUR

Let us suppose that the authorities have decided upon the real wage rate and the number of workers to be employed on investment. (We are abstracting from employment for other non-saleable output.) As we have just seen, the two decisions mutually entail each other when the capacity for producing saleable output is given.

We must now remove the assumption that there is only one technique of production known (only one possible kind of plough). This raises intricate problems and we must take them one by one.[1]

(i) *Superior techniques*. Using the terminology and other assumptions of the last exercise, suppose that there are two kinds of ploughs known, a 'heavy' and a 'light'. Considerably more work is required to build the heavy plough. Each is used by one man. Each is highly durable so that we need not bother about future replacements. The corn grown per plough-man-year is greater when the heavy plough is used.

How should the authorities decide which type of plough to build?

The first step is to find out whether one corn-growing technique is *superior* to the other in the sense that it yields a higher return both per unit of labour and per unit of investment.

Figure 5

This can be illustrated as follows. The product of a year's work of a team of plough-makers is ready for use. (As before, we abstract from the build-up of work in progress after equipment begins to be used,

[1] This group of exercises is stiffer than those attempted so far.

so that ploughs begin to yield corn immediately.) On the x axis measure the number of men offered employment in operating the new batch of ploughs. On the y axis measure the additional output of corn per year.

If all the new batch of ploughs were of the light type, a certain amount of labour would be offered employment and a certain future flow of output of corn produced. Mark the corresponding point in the labour-output space at L. From the point L draw a perpendicular to the y axis in L', and from the origin, O, draw a straight line through L. The height OL' represents the increment of output due to the given investment in the light technique and the slope of OL represents output per man employed. Produce $L'L$ and OL and mark the space lying above both with a plus sign and the space below with a minus. This leaves the triangle OLL' unmarked. Now enter in the diagram the point H which corresponds to the resulting output and employment when the whole batch of investment consists of the heavy equipment. H lies to the left of L, for fewer heavy than light ploughs are produced by the same investment (that is by a year's work of the same team of plough makers) and fewer men employed in ploughing. If H falls in the minus area showing that output per man is less than with the light technique, it is merely an aberration, for there is no object in making heavier equipment to get a smaller output. If H lies in the plus area the heavy technique is superior to the light. A given investment in heavy equipment not only yields a larger output per man employed (H lies above OL) but also makes a larger contribution to total output (H lies above $L'L$). Clearly, the light ploughs are a dud investment and should not be built.

There is no reason to scrap any light ploughs already in existence, however, for there is plenty of labour not yet employed to man up the new equipment as it is produced, and there is no point in depriving workers now using inferior techniques of employment and depriving the economy of their output.

It is to be observed that this investment in the heavy technique, though it offers less employment in ploughing than the light, generates a larger increase in total employment, for the surplus of corn over its own wages bill can be used to employ more workers in plough-making. This is because, in this exercise, the supply of commodities is the only limit upon employment, and whatever yields the largest increment in the flow of output of corn yields the largest increment of employment. It might be thought that this assumption is so unreal as to deprive the exercise of any interest, because equipment cannot be produced without the aid of equipment, and mere bodies with corn to feed them do not constitute investment potential. This is certainly true of modern industrial equipment, but there is a great deal of investment (irrigation schemes and road building are the classic examples) where extremely useful work can be done by labour with next to no equipment. In such cases only corn is needed to make investment possible.

(ii) *The degree of mechanisation.* Now consider the case where the 'heavy' technique yields a lower total increment of output (for the given investment) though a higher output per head. (H lies in the triangle OLL'.) Neither technique is superior to the other. The technique for using the heavy ploughs produces a larger output per man, but only at the expense of requiring a larger investment per man employed in ploughing. It is not superior to the technique with light ploughs but it is of a higher *degree of mechanisation*.

The degree of mechanisation cannot be measured quantitatively, but the possible techniques at the same level (neither superior nor inferior to each other) can be ranged in order of the output per head that they yield, that with a higher output per head being ranked as a higher degree of mechanisation. (Differences in durability complicate the argument. Here we are assuming all the ploughs to have an indefinitely long working life.)

A choice between techniques of different degrees of mechanisation (for a given amount of investment) means a choice between a larger output requiring more labour to produce it and a smaller output requiring less labour, that is between a larger total with less per head and a smaller total with more per head.

If the authorities can vary the wage rate, simply sharing the total output of consumption goods amongst the population, their obvious course is to choose the technique that offers the largest flow of output from the given investment. In this case they choose the light ploughs. A given investment then offers more employment than if heavy ploughs are chosen. It is to be observed, however, that employment is not an end in itself. It is the output which is the objective of policy. Otherwise any number of people could be employed on useless tasks.

(iii) *Output and surplus*. When the real wage rate has been set at a level below which it cannot be reduced, a worker called into the organised economy from the limbo of non-employment absorbs a definite quantity of consumer goods.

In such a case it is not at all obvious how the authorities should decide. Higher total output means higher employment and less misery in the immediate future. But it means lower output per head, and since they are committed to a certain real wage rate, lower output per head may mean a smaller increment of surplus available to expand investment and so a slower rate of acceleration (if not an actual deceleration) in the pace at which the non-employed are absorbed. The faster the rate of improvement in such a case, the greater the misery in the immediate future.

Figure 6

The problem can be illustrated as follows. Draw a fresh diagram with the same axes as the last one. H lies in the triangle OLL'. The straight line HL represents the variation of employment and output with the composition of the batch of ploughs. When all are of the heavy type we are at the point H. When the same plough-making labour has produced a batch all of the light type we are at L. As we move down the line from L to H the proportion of heavy ploughs increases and of light falls (for every heavy plough added, subtract the number of light ones produced by the same amount of plough-making labour). Consequently employment and output both fall from L to H.

Now draw a straight line from the origin representing the wage bill in terms of corn for the workers using the new batch of ploughs. Its slope represents the wage per man employed and the height of any point on it the total of wages paid for the corresponding amount of work in ploughing. The vertical distance between this line and HL is the total surplus. If the slope of this line is less than that of

HL there is no problem. The technique which yields the greater output also yields the greater surplus. The dilemma appears when the wage rate is such as to make the slope of the wage line greater than that of *HL*. In such a case, it can be seen that, as we move from *H* towards *L*, the increment of output due to greater employment is less than the increment of consumption of wages associated with it, so that where output is greatest (at *L*) the surplus over wages is least. (It may be negative. If the wage line cuts *HL* to the left of *L*, this means that, with the light ploughs, the increment of output due to the given batch of investment is less than the increment of wages, at the decreed rate, necessary to pay for the labour to operate the new equipment, so that the surplus that made this investment possible is eaten into, and next year the increment of equipment and employment will be less.)

Conversely, where output is least (at *H*) the surplus over wages is greatest, and consequently so is the contribution that can be made to speeding up investment.

On general grounds it seems that some kind of intermediate policy would be the best (assuming that the wage rate cannot be altered), but there is no one obviously right way of balancing the conflicting considerations and interests involved and the choice of technique, when it comes to the point, has to be settled by a political decision.

(iv) *Investment and waiting*. We must now contemplate a different kind of technical choice—that which concerns the time pattern of output. Let us suppose, now, that there are two kinds of ploughs, to be called 'hard' and 'soft' (instead of 'heavy' and 'light'). The difference between them is that the hard ploughs last much longer than the soft. To keep the argument as simple as possible, let us suppose that the hard ones retain their full efficiency indefinitely (they never need to be replaced) while the soft ones retain their full efficiency as long as they are usable at all and drop to pieces suddenly after a definite amount of wear (they belong to what is known as the *one-hoss-shay* type of equipment[1]).

Clearly, if the annual surplus of corn per unit of investment is the same whichever kind of plough is used, the soft type involves an inferior technique and it should never be built (any in existence can continue to be used and should be replaced by the hard type when they wear out).

The problem of choice arises when more can be built of the soft type by the same team of plough makers so that a given investment offers more employment in corn growing and a higher rate of output of corn next year. From the point of view of the immediate future it is superior, but a little later it will require to be replaced (absorbing the time of some plough-making workers who would otherwise be adding to the stock of equipment) while the hard plough is still working. To make the comparison between the two techniques fair we must deduct something from the output of the soft plough. As a first approximation, deduct an amount equal to its initial cost of production (the corn wage of the workers who built it) spread in instalments over its useful life. But this is overdoing the allowance, for the high output of its early years is worth more—ton for ton—than the corn-cost of

---

[1] 'Have you heard of the wonderful one-hoss shay,
That was built in such a logical way
It ran a hundred years to a day?'
Oliver Wendell Holmes: *The Deacon's Masterpiece*

replacing it later, because the surplus of its product over the wages bill for the workers required to operate it goes to support investment workers and so contributes to further production. To adjust the calculation for this the soft plough should be, so to speak, credited with interest on the instalments of its replacement cost, at a rate equal to the rate at which the annual output of corn (and therefore employment) is growing. On this basis the productivity in terms of corn over the indefinite future of the two techniques (hard and soft) can be compared. But this comparison is not enough to settle the choice between them. As well as the objective fact that corn now is worth more than corn in the future because it can be made productive meanwhile, there is also the subjective fact that corn, when it contributes to reducing the numbers of non-employed workers, is worth more (in diminution of misery) than can be measured by its physical productivity. In an economy with a large reserve of labour, therefore, there should be a bias in favour of quick-yielding investments even when they are somewhat less productive in physical terms than those which take longer to yield their first fruits.

(v) *Warning*. It is sufficiently obvious that the above exercises are scratching the surface of a very deep subject. Here it is more than ever necessary to pay careful attention to the restrictive assumptions which hedge the argument before drawing any conclusions from it. The same warning applies to the section which follows.

18. COSTS AND YIELD OF DEEPENING INVESTMENT[1]

We must now consider the socialist economy in conditions of full employment. All that we said, in the

[1] This section is difficult and may be postponed until the reader is feeling strong.

case of the family economy, about the burden of providing for a growing population, applies equally to the socialist economy. We may therefore take the relevant exercises as read and consider our fully employed socialist nation with constant population. We are still ruling out economies of scale, and we also neglect an interesting and important range of questions by assuming that the time to be worked per year by a fully employed man is rigidly fixed.

When we discussed accumulation in the family economy we assumed that all decisions were taken in concrete terms without going through any process of evaluation. With complicated processes of production carried out by great numbers of people who never meet each other, direct methods are not feasible; there has to be some system of accounting and some way of setting costs against benefits in order to control economic activity. Before going any further we must consider what costs and proceeds mean for the socialist nation.

The assumption of a 'one-commodity world' and of homogeneous labour clears out of the way many difficulties which will be taken up in Part Five. Meanwhile we continue to enjoy the benefit of these drastic simplifications.

(i) *Wages and marginal product*. The wages bill of the socialist enterprises is not a relevant measure of cost from the point of view of the economy as a whole. Wages are a means of imposing discipline and getting workers to work and they are a means of distributing saleable goods to the public, not a measure of cost.

It is easy to see the irrelevance of money wages by considering the following case. When accumulation continues after full employment has been reached productivity increases and it may be decided to permit an increased output of saleable goods. A sufficient effective demand to permit them to be distributed can be generated by reducing their prices, keeping money-wage rates constant; or by raising money-wage rates, keeping prices constant; or by any appropriate combination of the two. The choice of method has no significant effect except upon the number of money tokens required for circulation.

This is sufficiently obvious, but it is also true that the real-wage rate is no measure of social costs. When there were potential workers not employed and the corn-wage rate was unalterably fixed (on whatever principle it may have been chosen) corn was the final limiting factor upon output. With more corn there could be more employment and more production. But once full employment has been reached, it is labour itself that is the limiting factor. In the above case, where the real-wage rate is rising with growing productivity, there is obviously no sense in which the real cost of labour is growing. Indeed there is a certain sense in which it is falling, for it now costs progressively less human effort, as time goes by, to produce a given output.

There is, however, a real meaning to be given to the social cost of investment in terms of commodities. In a given situation with given means of production in existence (factories, mines, farms, etc., just as they happen to be at the moment) there is a certain product in the commodity sector of the economy for each amount of labour employed there (the assumption of a given 'basket' of products looks after the proportions in which different commodities must be produced). Then, when the total amount of labour allotted to commodity production has been decreed, there is a definite *short-period marginal product* of labour, being the amount by which output, in terms of 'baskets' of commodities, would be less if a small amount less of labour were employed, everything else being the same. (Please note that this definition is in terms of a difference, not of a change. The *fall* in output due to a *reduction* of employment is a more complicated concept.)

So far we have assumed that the capacity output of all means of production is quite rigid and that hours of work are given. In that case, any plant which is in use has a definite complement of workers. Plants may differ, however, in respect of the output per man which they yield. There is then a *marginal plant* for any given size of the labour force, being the plant which yields the lowest output per head. The marginal product of labour (at that size of the labour force) is then the average product in the marginal plant.

When there is some variability in the rate of output from given equipment, the maximum output from a given labour force (or the minimum labour for a given output) is attained when the distribution of workers over the plants is such as to equalise the marginal product of labour everywhere. The analysis is exactly the same as that which we used in discussing the disposition of the labour force over the area of a bowl of land (§(2)). When the margins are equalised, it is impossible to increase output by transferring a unit of labour from an older or less conveniently sited plant to a more efficient one, or by transferring a unit of labour from a plant being worked above its designed capacity to one which allows more elbow room. The marginal product of labour in each plant is then equal to the average product of labour in the marginal plant.

The relation of the real wage (which we take to be the same for all workers) to the marginal product of labour in the commodity sector depends upon the proportion of the labour force engaged in it.

Figure 7

This can be illustrated as follows. Take employment on the x axis and the flow of output of commodities (say, in 'baskets' per week) on the y axis. Draw the curve showing average product per head for different amounts of labour applied to the given productive capacity (the plant, etc.) in the commodity sector, and the corresponding curve of marginal productivity. The average curve is falling to the right (expressing conditions of short-period diminishing returns) so that the marginal curve lies below it.

OE, measured on the x axis, is the total amount of employment. OC (less than OE) is employment in the commodity sector. OW', measured on the y axis, is the wage per man week in terms of commodities. Then $OW'.OE$ is the total wage bill in terms of commodities. It is assumed that all wages are currently spent on commodities. Draw a perpendicular to the y axis at W' (the wage line) and a perpendicular to the x axis at C, to cut the wage line in W, the marginal productivity curve in M, and the average productivity curve in A. Then the flow of output of commodities is represented by the rectangle $OC.CA$, and this is equal to the wages bill $CW.OE$. It can readily be seen that (given the shape of the productivity curves) the greater is the ratio of CE to OE (the greater the proportion of the labour force engaged on non-saleable production) the greater is $CM–CW$ (the difference between the marginal product and the real wage).

The difference between the wage and the short-period marginal product of labour may go either way, according to the amount of surplus required to provide the wage for the workers engaged on non-saleable output. (This matter is further discussed in Part Five §11.)

(ii) *Social cost*. We can now return to the question of the social cost of investment. The short-period marginal product of labour in terms of commodities (or in terms of money of constant purchasing power over commodities) is a measure of the abstinence involved in employing labour on marginal investment. For instance, suppose that capacity is limited so that if more labour had been allotted to the production of commodities output would not have been much greater. The sacrifice of consumable output in putting labour to work on investment (or other non-saleable services) is then not very great. (This would be shown in the diagram by the average productivity curve falling steeply to right as it passes through the point A, so that CM is very small.) At the other extreme, if there is surplus capacity not being utilised so that average and marginal products are equal (M coincides with A) every addition to employment in the commodity sector would lead to a proportionate increase in output and so in the wage rate. The authorities have to weigh the advantages to be hoped from investment and other non-saleable production against the desire of the public for higher consumption immediately. (Here we are assuming hours of work fixed. If we remove this assumption, the cost of leisure can be analysed on similar lines.)

It is to be observed that work and abstinence are not two elements of real cost that can be added together. Work is being done in any case, and the abstinence consists in the loss of potential consumption due to work which is *not* being done in the commodity sector. There is no abstinence involved in investment made by labour that would otherwise not have been employed at all.

(iii) *The marginal efficiency of investment*. The benefit from investment when a given labour force is already fully employed must be sharply distinguished from the yield of investment when employment is increasing. When the existence of means of production makes it possible to employ labour which would otherwise not have been employed, the whole of the consequent product is, in a sense, due to the investment which brought the means of production into being. Similarly, when investment makes it possible to replace an inferior by a newly invented superior technique of production, the benefit of the technical progress involved is embodied in the yield of the investment. Here we are considering investment in a given state of technical knowledge, in the sense that there are no new inventions which make any existing technique inferior to the best known, and with a labour force which is in any case fully employed.

This raises problems considerably more complicated than those which arise when investment is widening the stock of equipment to provide for a growing labour force (discussed in §3).

As before, we begin by separating the characteristics of the technique of production concerned with the degree of mechanisation as with 'light' and 'heavy' ploughs (§17, ii), from those concerned with the time pattern of investment and output, as with 'soft' and 'hard' ploughs (§17, iv).

There are assumed to be various alternative methods of producing a given flow of output of commodities, requiring various amounts of investment per man employed, embodied in various kinds of 'machines' (corresponding to the 'ploughs' of our former example). When machines are being operated to produce commodities, each entails a particular amount of work in progress in the pipe-lines of production. This is included as part of the equipment for operating the technique in question.

We first consider a case in which the length of time taken to build a machine and get it into operation is the same for all types, and the length of time that each is expected to be used is the same. Thus we need not bother about the time pattern of production, but can compare techniques purely in terms of the cost of investment per man, cost being reckoned in terms of current output of consumer goods forgone.

The first step in the argument is, as before, to sort out inferior from superior techniques.

Figure 8

We can set up a diagram similar to the one in §17(i), but since employment is now the fixed quantity it is more convenient to draw it the other way round.

Take output per man in the commodity sector (say, in 'baskets' per week) on the y axis and the cost of investment per man on the x axis, with origin O, the cost of investment being reckoned in terms of man-hours of labour in the investment sector. One technique, say Beta, promises a particular output per man and requires a particular cost of equipment per man. Take OB on the y axis to represent the output and Ob on the x axis to represent the cost of equipment and let the perpendiculars from the axes at those points meet at the point β. The slope of the line $O\beta$ then represents output per unit of cost of equipment. Any point lying above

c

both $O\beta$ produced and $B\beta$ represents a technique
superior to Beta, and any point lying below $O\beta$ and
$B\beta$ produced represents a technique inferior to Beta.
A point lying in the left hand triangle, with a lower
output per man and a higher output per unit of cost
of equipment, represents a less mechanised technique,
and a point in the right hand triangle a more
mechanised technique (in our former examples, the
light ploughs represented a less mechanised technique
than the heavy ones). Testing each possible technique
in this way and rejecting inferior ones we, so to say,
map out the frontier representing the best techniques
known.

Let us suppose that there are three which pass the
test, Gamma, Beta and Alpha, represented in the
diagram by the points γ, β and α, with outputs
OC, OB and OA in ascending order on the y axis and
costs of equipment Oc, Ob and Oa along the x axis.

Comparing Gamma with Beta, an additional
output per man, CB, is the result of an additional
cost of equipment per man, cb. The slope of the $\gamma\beta$
line is the ratio of the additional output to the
additional cost. This ratio is the *marginal efficiency of
investment* at that point on the technical frontier.

Similarly the slope of $\beta\alpha$ represents the marginal
efficiency of investment at a higher degree of
mechanisation. The slope of $\beta\alpha$ is less than the slope
of $\gamma\beta$ (for as we move to the right along $\gamma\beta\alpha$ output
per unit of capital falls). This expresses the fact
that the marginal efficiency of investment falls off
as the degree of mechanisation already achieved
becomes greater.

It must be remembered that we are here discussing
a choice between techniques already known. There is
no reason to suppose that as a matter of history the

marginal efficiency of investment falls as the stock of equipment increases, for investment takes time and as time goes by technical progress is continuously making unforeseen changes in productivity. Our assumptions have ruled out unforeseen technical change only for the sake of the exercise.

The additional output due to investment (represented by *CB* or *BA* in the diagram) is a flow of baskets of commodities produced per week, and the additional cost (*cb* or *ba*) is a sum reckoned in terms of commodities forgone. The ratio between them can then be represented as a proportional rate per unit of time, and expressed as so much per cent per annum, like a rate of interest or a rate of profit. (It is, however, rather a dangerous habit to express the marginal efficiency of investment as a rate of interest, or the other way round, as a capital to output ratio, for there are important differences between the *realised money* return on a *stock* and the *real* return to be *expected* from an *addition* to productive equipment. Moreover, we are considering the marginal efficiency of investment from the point of view of the economy as a whole, whereas profit and interest are usually associated with the incomes of private capitalists.)

(iv) *The cost of waiting.* We must now introduce the problem of the choice between techniques with different time patterns.

An investment which begins to yield earlier is superior in an objective sense, quite apart from human impatience, to one, otherwise equal, which has a longer gestation period, for the proceeds of the quick yielding investment can in turn be invested (that is to say that labour can be transferred from the consumption to the investment sector) and a larger flow of output produced by the time that the slow yielding one is ripe, with no loss of consumption meanwhile.

Thus if, in a particular situation, an investment of 100 units to-day will yield a permanent increase of output of 10 units per annum beginning after one year, it is not inferior to an investment which will begin to yield 11 units after two years, for the first investment, without any further cut in consumption, could be made to yield 11 units after two years, by reinvestment of the first 10 of product.

The marginal efficiency of a quicker yielding investment thus measures the cost of waiting for a slower-yielding one.

This is the cost of waiting for the yield of an investment, measured in terms of the potential output of commodities forgone. A human preference for present consumption over a perfectly confident expectation of an equally satisfying consumption later (discount of the future), an expectation that times will be easier in the future, so that abstinence is felt to be more onerous now than it will be later (falling marginal utility of income) and the feeling that a bird in the hand is worth two in the bush (uncertainty of future income) add a subjective burden of waiting which may well influence investment plans, but these imponderable elements are not included in our definition of the objective cost of waiting.

(v) *Obsolescence*. We also have to consider the period of future time over which an investment is expected to yield. This is not a simple question, for it partly depends upon the rate at which investment is going on.

As we have seen (§17(iv)), so long as there is labour available to be absorbed into employment the working life of plant is as long as it can be made to hold together, but when all labour is already employed, new plant can be manned only by taking labour from old. As each new batch of plant becomes ready for use labour has to be found to man it, and (to maximise total production) labour must be taken away from the points where its output is least, and the plant denuded of labour must be scrapped, whatever its physical condition. Plant becomes obsolete not because of any change in itself but because more productive plant has become available. To concentrate the question, let us suppose that all equipment is highly durable (like land) and could retain its full physical efficiency for an indefinitely long working life. Then no scrapping is due to mere age and all is due to obsolescence.

As investment is going on, providing an ever 'deeper' stock of means of production for a given labour force, the short-period marginal product of labour is gradually rising. As the short-period marginal product of a given amount of labour is raised, the gross surplus being yielded by old plant is reduced.

Figure 9

This can be illustrated by drawing a series of diagrams of the same form as that in §18(i) for single plants, with the average productivity curve of each starting from the y axis at a different point. Some may be box-shaped curves, horizontal up to a corner and then falling vertically, indicating that the short-period marginal product of labour is equal to average product up to capacity output, and that capacity is quite rigid. For plants represented by these curves there is no change in utilisation until they are scrapped (*a fortiori* if marginal product rises up to capacity, as may be the case in some technical conditions). For others the marginal product rises gradually as the amount of labour employed falls, and labour may be taken away from them (to man new plant) in a series of instalments (*OC* falls as *CM* rises).

As the short-period marginal product of labour in the commodity sector as a whole rises, the surplus (*AM.OC* in the diagram) on each plant falls, and one after the other comes on to the 'extensive margin' where it yields no surplus at all.

These diagrams can be used only to compare positions with different values of marginal productivity, but the succession of positions indicates the movement through time with some complications omitted.

When a particular plant is in the position of yielding no surplus over the short-period marginal product of labour, it is due to be scrapped and its labour fitted up with the newest plant, which yields the highest surplus. In this constant game of leap-frog, a particular plant moves from the first to the last position the more rapidly, and therefore has a shorter service life (other things equal), the more rapidly the short-period marginal productivity of labour is rising, that is, the faster investment is going on relatively to the total of labour employed.

(vi) *A difficult question*. The calculations concerned with the time pattern of investments are, in principle, quite simple (though the mathematics is elaborate) provided that they can be conducted in terms of a single definite rate of marginal efficiency which is expected to rule as far ahead as the planning authorities care to look. If there is such a single marginal efficiency of investment, it can be used as a measure of the cost of waiting, and expressed as a rate of discount to be applied to all future costs and future returns. On this basis, the discounted present value of all schemes of investment can be calculated and compared. But the marginal efficiency of investment varies, at any moment, with the scale of investment that is being planned, and when deepening investment is going on (with a constant labour force and no technical progress) the marginal efficiency of investment will be falling as time goes by. When the marginal efficiency of investment is expected to change in the future it cannot be expressed as a single interest rate. It splits, like light passing through a prism, into a spectrum of interest rates applicable to the range of future time. Thus, if the general level of these interest rates is expected to fall over the future, the rates applicable to shorter terms are higher than those for longer terms.

This not only makes calculation impossibly complicated, but also raises some conceptual difficulties about the very meaning of the marginal efficiency of investment.

Here we are in deeper water than these exercises are intended to plumb. For our present purposes we must be content with a crude treatment of these subtle questions, and we shall continue to talk of the marginal efficiency of investment and the cost of waiting without being too scrupulous about their precise specification.

19. AN INVESTMENT PROGRAMME

We now consider a socialist economy which, having reached full employment, is continuing to invest in deepening productive capacity.

A policy decision has to be taken as to how the real wage rate in terms of commodities is to behave as output per head rises. If real wages are kept constant, labour is gradually withdrawn from the commodity

sector as productivity there rises, and drafted over to
non-saleable production. If labour in the commodity
sector is kept constant, the real wage rate rises with
the average product of labour. If the rate of investment
slackens off (or other non-saleable production is
reduced) so that more labour is drafted into the
commodity sector, the wage rate rises more than in
proportion to average product. (These relations can be
illustrated by means of the short-period diagram,
§18(i).)

The way in which the socialist nation chooses to
take advantage of rising productivity is a matter of
policy which has to be decided on general grounds.
As we saw in discussing the Gee family (§12), there is
no purely economic criterion by which the one and only
right policy can be found. The simplest case to take for
an exercise is that in which the amount of labour in
the commodity sector is kept constant, and wages rise
with output per head. The labour force in the investment
sector is then also constant. We assume that investment-
sector labour is already provided with equipment
which is versatile and can be used to make various
kinds of machines for the consumption sector. The
investment-sector workers keep their own equipment
intact. (These assumptions provide us with a simple
exercise, but it must be noticed that they rule out a
large part of the difficulties that face actual investment planners.)

When the rate of investment has been decided, it is
possible to calculate the length of service life of each
type of equipment (§18(v)) and to reckon the marginal
efficiency of investment in each type.

Let us suppose that, when our story begins, the
consumption sector is equipped with Gamma type
machines, and that, for the time being, Beta shows the

highest marginal efficiency. (This is represented in the diagram by the slope of $\gamma\beta$, which is greater than that of $\gamma\alpha$.)

Beta equipment gradually replaces Gamma in the consumption-sector, and average output per man rises. In terms of the short-period diagram (§18(i)) drawn to illustrate the situation at any moment while this process is going on, there is a step in the marginal productivity curve; up to the number of men equipped for Beta technique it is at the average Beta level, and beyond this drops to the Gamma level. In successive periods the corner in the curve moves to the right, as the number of men equipped for the higher rate of output increases.

The prospective life of a Beta machine grows shorter as the date at which Alpha equipment will begin to be installed comes nearer, and after a certain point has been reached, Beta becomes inferior to Alpha, so that it becomes preferable to replace the remaining Gamma machines with Alpha ones.

To use the diagram to illustrate the choice of technique we must redraw it at each moment when a choice has to be made. As time goes by and output per head rises, the cost of an item of investment in terms of commodities forgone increases. At the same time the cost of waiting falls. The positions of the points representing the various techniques therefore shifts, and the course of the marginal efficiency of investment, though it must in general be downwards, cannot be expected to follow a smooth and regular path.

This analysis, in spite of our highly abstract assumptions, is quite complicated, but it is a very faint reflection of the actual difficulties that beset authorities in charge of drawing up investment plans.

20. THE APPROACH TO BLISS

To contemplate an economy reaching bliss may be considered an enervating kind of Utopian daydreaming, but it provides a convenient way of dealing with certain concepts which are useful in other contexts.

Let us suppose that Alpha technique, in the last example, is the most mechanised known. We will now assume that Alpha plant is not perfectly durable but has a definite life at full efficiency (the 'one-hoss-shay' assumption). We continue for the moment to assume that the amount of work done in the commodity and investment sectors taken together remains constant, and we abstract from investment for amenities and all non-saleable production. When the original labour force of the commodity sector is all equipped with Alpha machines, the rate of investment will begin to decline, and labour released from investment can be absorbed into the commodity sector. Men are drawn out of the investment sector as fast as machines can be provided to equip them. The real wage rate continues to rise after the maximum output per head has been reached. (In the short-period diagram, the point C moves to the right, while CA remains constant, OE is constant, CE falling and CW rising.)

The decline in employment in the investment sector comes to an end when the current output of Alpha machines is only just enough to make good those which wear out (there may have to be a series of wobbles in employment in the investment sector until the age-composition of the stock of machines is stabilised).

In this situation the marginal efficiency of investment is zero. The cost of waiting is zero (all the waiting that is of any use has been done already). There is, however, still a sense in which there may be said to be some abstinence going on, for it would be possible to increase consumption immediately by drawing workers out of the investment sector (after building some Beta machines for them to operate) thus reducing future productive capacity or, as the phrase is, 'consuming capital'. Refraining from doing so may be regarded as a kind of abstinence. (This corresponds to the second type of stationary state mentioned in §8.)

It is somewhat unnatural to think of approaching bliss with a constant amount of work being done. Let us remove this assumption and allow our socialist economy to enjoy part of the benefit of rising productivity in the form of increasing leisure. This means that as output per head rises during the period when Alpha machines are gradually superseding Beta, the real wage rate rises by less (in the short-period diagram, OC falls as CA rises; therefore CW rises less than in proportion to CA). If extra leisure is taken in the form of shorter hours (with single shift working) the amount of plant required is no less than in the former case, and if the number of workers in each sector remains the same, bliss will take longer to reach. If leisure takes the form of a smaller working force (some bodies at any moment being on holiday or at the university) the total plant required is less, and with an equal proportionate reduction in work in each sector, bliss is reached in the same time as when leisure is not increased.

21. INVENTIONS AND DISCOVERIES

In order to isolate the problems connected with 'deepening' investment, we have assumed that all possible techniques were already known. But in reality there is a built-in tendency to technical progress in an industrial economy.

As time goes by the personal efficiency of workers increases, so that output per head with given equipment rises. Moreover, some part of the non-saleable activity of the economy is devoted to research and experiment, and this throws up a continuous stream of improvements which can be embodied in new plant as it is produced. A regular stream of improvements can be foreseen and allowed for in the investment programme, newly discovered superior techniques being embodied in plant at the same time as the degree of mechanisation is raised, so that output per head rises, as time goes by, for both reasons together.

If the real wage is held constant, technical progress permits a faster rate of accumulation to be carried out, for labour released by it from producing commodities can be drafted into investment. When the division of the labour force between the sectors is kept constant, technical progress contributes to raising the real wage rate.

From time to time, large unforeseen discoveries redraw the whole picture and require the investment programme to be radically reconsidered. Technical progress, like a growth of population, makes it impossible ever to reach bliss.

PART TWO

ACCUMULATION AND DISTRIBUTION

I. FACTOR INCOMES

BEFORE we can discuss a full-blown capitalist economy we must see the effect of introducing private property in the means of production into our exercises, and we will first treat it in terms of a non-monetary economy, in which bargains can be arranged and payments made in terms of consumable goods.

I. AN ECONOMY OF FREEHOLDERS

Let us imagine once more a fertile, uniform plain (as in Part One §1) and people it with a number of families, each owning a limited amount of land. If each works its own land with whatever labour its members are able and willing to provide, the distribution of labour over the area as a whole is quite haphazard. Some families who happen to have a high ratio of land to labour enjoy a relatively high level of production and consumption per head. They find the marginal product of land very low and the marginal product of labour high. Others are in the reverse position.

We assume that none is carrying out any real investment simply because they do not know of anything to do in the way of improving their means of production; all the same, there may be lending and borrowing amongst them. Some families which are poor, spendthrift or unlucky from time to time borrow consumption goods from those better off or more thrifty, promising to repay with a premium and pledging their land as security. The rate of premium for such transactions settles itself from day to day as the balance shifts to and fro between the volume of demand for present consumption against future payments and the volume of demand for future income against present abstinence. There is a strong tendency for the rich to grow richer, as time goes by, and the poor to grow poorer, but the appearance of spendthrifts from time to time in wealthy families, and heroic frugality in poor families, may set a brake upon the process of concentration of wealth that is going on.

2. LAND AND LABOUR WITHOUT CAPITAL

Now let us suppose that the system is so organised that individuals can work on land that does not belong to their own families. Some of the families with excess workers hire land, and some of those with excess land hire workers, which takes the initiative being a matter of chance.

We will again suppose that no investment is going on in means of production (no land drainage, more ploughs, extra seed corn, etc.) and that every worker is already equipped with any implements he needs.

All concerned are assumed to operate on strict economic principles and the hire-prices of the factors are settled by supply and demand. Any family is willing to hire labour as long as the marginal product of labour on their land exceeds the hire-price. And any one is willing to hire land so long as the marginal product of land with the labour that they are able and willing to provide, exceeds the rent they must pay for the land. Any one is willing to go out to work provided that what he is promised as pay is not less than the marginal product of the work on his own family's land; and any family is willing to let land provided the rent is not less than the product that their own labour could produce on it. At any moment, if the level of rent that happens to be ruling is less than the marginal product of land to any family, that family will be bidding for more land; and if the hire-price of labour is less than the marginal product of labour to any family, that family will be bidding for more workers. In a state of *equilibrium*, in which everyone is satisfied that he could not better himself by a change, the marginal productivities of land and of labour are each equal over the whole area. The maximum possible product is then being produced for the economy as a whole and the hire-price of each factor has settled at the level which corresponds to its marginal product.

Figure 10(a)

This can be illustrated as follows. Draw a diagram, similar to that which we drew for the one-family economy, or to our short-period diagram, showing the marginal and average product of different amounts of labour with the available amount of land. Mark *OC* as the total amount of labour in the economy. Then the equilibrium hire-price of labour is *CM*, the marginal product of *OC* labour. *CA* is the average product per man. *AM.OC* is the marginal product of land multiplied by the total amount of land in the economy.

Figure 10(b)

Draw the same diagram the other way up, showing marginal and average product of different amounts of land with the available amount of labour. Mark *OL* as the actual amount of land. *LM*, the marginal product of *OL* land, is the rent of hired land and

AM.OL is the marginal product of labour multiplied by the total labour force.[1]

With equilibrium hire-prices ruling, the incomes of individuals may differ widely, depending upon how much land their families own, and, as in the last exercise, there may be a gradual drift towards concentration of wealth going on.

The equality of marginal products with hire prices entails that payments are made out of the product of the services hired. Since production takes time, a worker who goes out for hire is paid after a delay equal to the gestation period of the product to which his work has contributed. This means that he has to be supported by his family over the gestation period of the first round of production to which he contributes. Or, to look at the same thing in another way, the families supplying land are lending the land to those who work it and the families supplying labour are lending work to those who employ them, in each case taking payment in arrears when the product accrues.

3. THE WAGE FUND

An economy such as that described above, in which relations between landowners and workers are perfectly symmetrical, could exist only in very peculiar conditions for there is an important asymmetry between land and labour arising from the need that men have to eat every day. The daily consumption of workers cannot come out of their own product (at least since mankind ceased to rely entirely on hunting for food) and has to be provided from production already completed. Now, it is poor families who own little land (if any) whose members must go out to work, and they

[1] A formal proof of this relationship involves Euler's theorem. See Wicksell *Lectures*, Vol. I, pp. 124-130.

are not in a good position to lend work for long periods. This gives rise to the possibility of the system in which an employer of labour *finances* production by paying wages in advance of receiving proceeds, the workers being paid at intervals, of, say, a week or a month, which are short in relation to the gestation period of products. To set up as an employer, therefore, it is necessary to have access to liquid wealth—in the case of our non-monetary economy, a flow of output of ready-consumable goods. By employing labour at wages an employer invests this liquid finance in a wage fund.

Figure 11

The build-up of a wage fund can be illustrated by a figure similar to that which we used for the quantity of money. The wage bills of successive weeks are set side by side from the moment when work begins to the moment when the product emerges. In a simple case where work is done at an even rate and the product emerges in an even flow after, say, six months, the wage fund is half a year's wage bill, or twenty-six times a week's wage bill. More complex patterns can be illustrated in the same way.

4. PROFIT AND INTEREST

Let us now postulate that all the finance for workers is provided by employers, while rents are paid in arrears, so that no need for finance arises in the hiring of land. (We are neglecting variations in weather, which may give rise to the need for finance in sub-average years.)

The amount of employment that can be offered, at any given wage rate in terms of product, depends upon the amount of finance available. Finance, in general, will not be forthcoming unless it can secure a *profit*, that is, an excess of product over the payments made to the factors of production. This means that the level of wages must be less than that which would absorb the whole product after paying rent, so as to leave a margin to permit profit to be obtainable.

When profits are obtainable by employing labour, the provision of finance becomes a source of income, independently of organising employment. When a would-be employer does not command finance of his own, he is willing to hire finance provided that he does not have to pay more for it than the difference between the product of the labour which it enables him to employ and the wage (that is, provided it does not eat up the whole profit). In order to be able to hire finance the employer has to command credit, that is, he has to be able to satisfy lenders that he is a good borrower, who will be able to fulfil his undertakings. The hire price of finance is *interest*.

There is an important difference between this hire price and the others. Rent is so much product per acre, say, per year (paid, we have assumed, in arrears). A wage is so much product per man-hour of work (paid at short intervals). Interest is so much product per unit of product borrowed. It is expressed, therefore, as a fraction, a ratio, a pure number—so much per cent, per unit of time, instead of as a quantity of product per unit of factor, per unit of time.

5. FINANCE

There is something rather mysterious about finance. Let us imagine that we can watch a bit of it coming into existence for the first time, so that we can see what it is really like.

Let us begin when the process of bringing surplus labour and surplus land together has not been completed, and let us suppose that amongst the families in the economy there is one which consists of a single elderly man, who finds himself in possession of an area of land which he is not able or willing to work. Another family is very large, has little land, a very low income per head and a zero marginal product of labour on their own land. A third family is pretty comfortable. Now, one member of the last decides to seek his fortune independently of the rest of the family. He engages with the land-owner to pay rent for the loan of his land; he borrows from the well-to-do family, against a promise of interest, some product with which to pay wages, and sets some men from the second family to work on the land. If there are discrete annual harvests the lenders must have a stock of produce in their barns over and above what they intend to consume that year, which is available to serve as finance, but if production is continuous the finance does not need to exist physically all at one moment. They promise to lend what will be needed to their enterprising scion (for he has been able to inspire them with confidence in his ability to pay) and each week they hand over an amount of product equal to his wage bill, out of the surplus of their own production over their consumption. They are at the same time *saving* (consuming less than their income) and lending. The outstanding loan accumulates from week to week.

Assuming that the technical conditions of production are such that after a certain time a steady flow of output begins to emerge, the employer begins at the end of the first gestation period to pay wages out of the product of the workers whom he is employing, and he ceases to accumulate any further debt. He begins also to pay rent for the land. The employer now has command over *capital* equal to the wage fund that he borrowed, against which he owes a debt to the lenders, who have become *rentiers*. Assuming that he is operating on a scale that satisfies him, no more saving is needed, so far as he is concerned, from now on. The loan continues to exist as a financial counterpart to the real capital represented by the work in progress, which from now on exists as a constant self-reproducing stock, giving off a flow of output. The rentier family, if they wish to, can sell the debt to some other savers, and dissave their financial capital by consuming the proceeds, or re-lend it to someone else, without the real capital (the work in progress) being affected. The employer, if he wants to at some later date, can disinvest his real capital by gradually dismissing workers and ceasing to renew the process of production while output continues to flow out. He can then repay the original debt, or become a rentier by lending to an employer and receiving interest (from which he must pay interest to the first rentier). Thus, once a finance fund is in existence it can be swopped around amongst individuals who had nothing to do with the saving which created it in the first place.

The basic relations are the same when finance is committed to improvements of land, buildings, equipment, etc., provided by an employer to increase the productivity of his workers, but this *fixed capital* introduces some complications which we reserve for treatment in terms of an advanced capitalist economy.

6. COMPOUND INTEREST

The exact amount of the debt which the employer owes to the rentiers is a rather complicated matter. If they had not lent to him they could have taken over a debt to some one else, who was already paying interest. Therefore they can demand interest from the first moment that they begin to lend. (We are assuming that they have forgotten family feeling and are acting on strictly economic principles.) The employer cannot yet begin to pay, so the interest is added to the debt and claims interest in its turn. Thus when payment begins it is payment on the sum actually borrowed *plus* compound interest on each instalment of the debt for the length of time that it has been outstanding.

This is analogous to the cost of waiting which we have already come across (Part One §18, iv), but it is not the same thing, for it concerns financial transactions between individuals, not technical relations between work and production.

7. WAGES, RENT, INTEREST AND PROFIT

To employ labour is both troublesome and risky. Troublesome because the work has to be organised, and risky because finance has been borrowed and the possibility of paying the interest on it depends upon the expected product emerging from the process of production without any unfortunate accidents. Thus the profit expected from capital (that is from finance which has been committed to a process of production) must exceed the interest paid for the loan of finance corresponding to it. (Even if the employer is operating with funds that he owns himself this is still true, for he could obtain interest on this finance from someone else if he did not use it himself.)

The extent of this excess depends upon the number of would-be employers who command enough credit to be able to borrow, and upon their eagerness to engage in enterprise and their optimism about the risks involved.

The levels of the rate of interest and of real wages are interdependent. The level of wages is governed by the productivity of labour and the amount of finance available to offer employment in relation to the number of workers seeking employment. This is because, in the conditions that we have postulated, if wages and the rate of interest were such that very great profits could be made by borrowing finance and employing labour, employers, eager to get hands, would bid up wages. This both reduces prospective profits and increases the amount of finance required to employ a given amount of labour. Conversely, if labour were looking for employment, wages would be bid down, profits would be higher and finance per worker reduced. For equilibrium to be established, the wage rate must be that at which the available finance employs the available labour. Given the real wage rate and technical conditions, the rate of profit on capital is determined; the rate of interest must fall short of the rate of profit by whatever margin is required to induce employers to take the risk and trouble involved in operating with the capital. (We are assuming that the wage rate so determined is at least high enough to support the workers at a tolerable standard of life.)

The level of rents depends upon the supply of land available, given the amount of labour and technical conditions. A given amount of labour operating on a larger amount of land produces somewhat more product—the marginal product of the extra land from the point of view of the employer. This additional product is what the employer finds it worthwhile to pay for the land rather than have to operate with less. The greater the amount of labour working over the whole area (given technical conditions) the greater the intensity of utilisation of land at any point, and therefore the greater its marginal product to any individual employer and the higher the level at which rents settle.

We have postulated that there is no scope for investment to increase productivity. When all the available labour is working and when competitive bidding for land and labour has led to the labour being deployed over the land in such a way that its marginal productivity is everywhere equal, the maximum possible output is being produced in the economy as a whole.

Any further saving would merely lead to an increase in the amount of rentier wealth in existence and so to an increase in the funds that rentiers are willing to lend to employers. A competitive bidding down of the rate of interest would increase the margin of profit to employers and so lead to a bidding up of the real-wage rate. With a higher wage rate a larger fund of finance is required for a given amount of employment. Thus any additional finance could get itself absorbed with an appropriate reduction in the rate of interest.

The economy sinks into stationary equilibrium when the rate of interest is such that no one feels it worth while to own any more wealth, so that saving comes to an end. The wage rate is at the level which requires all the finance in existence to employ the available labour. The whole flow of product is being consumed by the recipients of the four types of income, wages, rents, interest and the excess of profit over interest. (The position is analogous to that of the Esse family in stationary conditions, Part One §9.)

This is quite unlike any situation found in reality, but the exercise is a useful one for searching out the basis of the relations between work, enterprise and property as sources of income.

8. A FALSE SCENT

What is the relation of these incomes to the marginal products of the factors of production? With the assumptions that we have been working on—no investment in implements, stationary conditions, etc.—there is no ambiguity about the meaning of the marginal physical products of the factors from the point of view of the economy as a whole, and competition for factors ensures that in equilibrium the marginal product of a factor from the point of view of an individual employer is equal to its marginal product to the economy as a whole. In the foregoing exercises when we changed over from mutual hiring to a system where employers finance wages, nothing was altered in technical conditions. When the whole available labour force is deployed over the available land in such a way as to maximise the total output of the economy, the marginal physical products of labour and of land, from the point of view of the economy as a whole, are given and are in no way affected by the manner in which the factors are hired.

We have supposed that rent absorbs the whole marginal product of land, because the landowner finances the use of his land by taking payment in arrears, so that an employer who hires land does not have to incur any interest charges in connection with it, and we suppose that a landowner could earn profits if he wanted to and will not accept any deduction from rent on account of being spared the bother of organising its use himself.

It can easily be seen from the pair of diagrams which we last drew, that if rent is equal to the marginal product of land from the point of view of the economy as a whole, the marginal product of labour must be equal to wages plus profits per man employed.

A great deal of confusion has been caused in economic theory, first by asserting that wages tend to equal the marginal product of labour from the point of view of the economy as a whole. The fact is overlooked that, even when there is no fixed capital, the product accruing to an employer must cover profit on the capital embodied in the wages fund, as well as the wages bill itself, while, when there is fixed capital, the marginal product of labour cannot be separated from that of the equipment it uses except in a short-period sense (as we saw in Part One §7).

Secondly, confusion is caused by introducing amorphous concepts such as the 'supply of waiting' or the 'supply of risk bearing' and treating them as though they were solid and measurable factors of production, like land and labour, with physical marginal products of their own.

It is true that the marginal *net* return on employing labour must be equal to the wage in equilibrium, in the sense that the additional product to be expected by an individual employer from additional employment, *minus* the interest cost of finance embodied in the wages fund for that amount of employment and *minus* an allowance of profit for the trouble and risk involved, is equal to the wage when equilibrium conditions prevail. But this is merely a restatement of the meaning of equilibrium as a position where no employer wants to employ any more or any less labour than he is actually doing. It does not assert that wages are equal to the value of the marginal physical product of labour from the point of view of society. Rather it draws attention to the fact that wages must be less than this to allow a margin for interest and profit.

II. A CAPITALIST ECONOMY

THERE are many interesting exercises to be done in working out the development of industrial capitalism from the embryo shown in the last section, but here we jump ahead and consider capitalism when it is full blown. To make the exercises manageable we draw a highly stylised picture of a pure capitalist system. We retain the 'one-commodity' assumption and we treat of a closed economy. All the production we shall consider is of saleable output and the investment connected with it. We abstract from the activities of government and pay no heed to the work that a family does for its own use. To lighten the argument we drop land as a separate factor of production—we may assume that of mere space there is no lack and that effective economic land can be created by investment just like any other means of production. We continue to assume labour homogeneous.

9. FIRMS AND HOUSEHOLDS

In our model of a capitalist economy there is a sharp division between business and private life. The citizens are organised in *firms* for business and in *households* for private life. The firm is a development of the employer of the last section, now operating not only a wages fund but much fixed capital as well. The fixed capital is organised in *plants*, each plant employing a large number of workers, equipped with buildings, machinery, etc. Some plants are designed for the production of commodities and some for the production of plants. A firm may operate any number of plants and any kind of plant.

A plant has a fairly definite productive capacity, given the normal hours of work, and we assume that there is a particular level of employment beyond which the short-period marginal physical product of labour in a given plant falls off very sharply. (This assumption is not basic to the analysis but helps to make it neat and easy to describe.)

The firm (like our first employer) may owe interest to rentiers who have lent to it on *bonds*, or it may have been provided with finance by *shareholders* in return for a promise of profit instead of a fixed interest. We shall treat shareholders as a kind of rentier, for like rentiers their only function is to put up finance and draw an income from it. The firm may also have provided itself with finance out of its own profits—legally, this belongs to the shareholders and represents saving-plus-lending that they have been induced to do. We ignore intermediate types of securities such as preference shares and indirect lending through deposits in banks which finance firms.

The firms have taken on certain human characteristics—desire for survival, ambition, emulation. (We see the same in many institutions, for instance, colleges or regiments. To probe the causes of this phenomenon would carry us into deep waters. Here we just accept it as a fact.) The managers of the firms identify themselves with the firm as such, and though they are legally the employees of the shareholders, they subject the shareholders' interests to what they regard as the interests of the firm as such (with which their own egos are bound up).

Transactions between firms—one selling raw materials to another, etc.—do not interest us at this stage. (They will be discussed in Part Four.) We can imagine each firm as completely integrated or we can simply cancel out all inter-firm transactions when we are discussing the relations of firms as a whole with households as a whole. Outgoings of firms then consist of wages paid to workers and interest and dividends paid to rentiers. These two classes of families constitute the households. We treat the managers of the firms as disembodied spirits who have no households of their own and we abstract from all sorts of professions, artisans, etc.

The households make payments to the firms for goods purchased—that is for commodities which are sold to them through shops. We assume that workers' families spend the whole of their wages currently as they receive them and that they have no borrowing power, so that they cannot spend more. Rentier families are free to spend either more or less in any period than they receive in that period.

When, over any period, the outpayments of the firms, taken as a whole, exceed their receipts, they are borrowing from the rentiers, in one form or another, so increasing their indebtedness, and when their receipts exceed their outpayments, they are gaining capital from the rentiers and reducing their indebtedness. The former situation is the normal one, for it is what occurs when finance borrowed from outside the firms is being embodied in capital, as in the case of the employer whom we examined in the last section. In the reverse case, rentiers taken as a whole are dissaving, which is a somewhat morbid state of affairs.

10. THE MAINSPRING

The firms are in a constant restless state of activity, each trying to grow at the expense of the others. To do so, they invest in more productive capacity and at the same time they try to increase output per unit of outlay, that is, to reduce costs. As each strives to resist the pressure of the others, net growth for the system as a whole results from their struggles. Some are more progressive than others, and set the pace. The pressure of competition from these progressive firms drives others to copy their methods, and so productivity is increased all round.

From this turmoil emerges a certain net rate of investment and a certain net rate of rise of output per head which is not any one's plan but happens blindly. The greater the energy, ingenuity and boldness of the firms, the faster the rate of net investment that emerges from their collective activities.

The above formulation represents my own view of what is the least unrealistic treatment of the subject of the inducement to invest. Other model-makers prefer to tie up the decision to invest with the rate of profit expected *ex ante*. (As we shall see, the rate of profit realised *ex post* is largely determined by the rate of investment, so that on that line cause and effect are not easy to keep apart.) On the view here adopted, the level at which the expected rate of profit normally runs does not affect the normal rate of accumulation of capital, but any fall in profits below the rate experienced in the past is liable to discourage investment and any rise to speed it up.

In our model, the rentiers are free, within limits, to vary their level of expenditure (which affects the level of profits), and they may be less or more willing to lend to firms (which affects the cost of borrowing). Through these channels they have a certain indirect influence on the rate of accumulation, but in the main their role is a passive one.

The workers may have a strong influence upon the level of money wages, but, given their personal efficiency, only an indirect influence on the level of real wages. They may, however, take a view as to the minimum tolerable level of real wages and refuse to accept employment below that level.

On this view, it is the operations of the firms that are the main determinant of development in the model of a pure capitalist system without any influence coming from government.

Other model-builders prefer other systems, for instance, one in which the decisions to save by rentiers play a dominating role in the determination of investment. The choice of model depends partly upon its convenience for the particular problems under discussion and partly upon judgment as to its resemblance to actual economic systems. The model here set up, in which the struggle of firms to survive and grow is the mainspring of development and the other classes only set limits within which it must operate, appears to me to be both the least unrealistic and the most convenient for conducting exercises on economic development and the distribution of income.

II. TECHNICAL PROGRESS

The success of capitalism is bound up with technical progress. If an employer had no more to offer than finance of a wages fund the system could easily dissolve into self-employment. In fact the economies of division of labour when a large group of workers is organised in a single enterprise, and the development of elaborate machinery involving complicated scientific principles, so much raise the productivity of workers whose employer commands a large amount of capital that self-employed workers cannot survive in competition with them.

These advanced techniques are pioneered one after another in the competitive struggle between firms. We did some exercises on a socialist economy before attempting capitalism because a planned economy is much easier to understand, but historically it is anomalous to do so; in reality socialism came into existence only after capitalism had developed a high level of technique. The 'deepening' investment which the socialist economy was doing in our exercises was catching up on methods of production, now well-known, that were once the latest superior techniques thrown up in the evolution of competition amongst capitalist firms.

Technical progress is one more very complicated subject which we must severely simplify for the purpose of our exercises.

We assume that there is a clear-cut distinction between the sector of the economy producing commodities and the sector producing equipment (though one firm may operate plants in both sectors) and that the ratio of investment in work-in-progress to investment in equipment (both measured in terms of labour time) never varies, so that we can treat the accumulation of productive capacity in terms solely of equipment.

Technical progress may take the form of increases in productivity due to increased efficiency of labour and management, so that it applies immediately to plant already in existence and has no effect on the design of new plant. When such improvements operate uniformly throughout the economy, output per head increases in both sectors uniformly. With constant employment, the rate of output of machines is speeded up, and the same workers are now able to manage more machines, producing the same output per machine and so more output per head.

More commonly, technical progress is embodied in new types of equipment. We then have to measure output per head in the investment sector in units of productive capacity in the commodity sector, and, when the investment sector is several layers deep, in output per head in the sector making machines to make machines for the commodity sector in units of productive capacity of machine-making equipment, and so on downwards.

When technical progress is going on, the latest equipment is superior to that installed last year, which in turn is superior to that installed the year before, and so on. Thus, if output per head is rising, say, at a rate of 2 per cent per annum and the length of life of a piece of equipment is five years, each item will be replaced after five years by one which yields somewhat more than 10 per cent higher rate of output per head. The next to be replaced will be 2 per cent better than that which was replaced this year. Thus a continuous leap-frog proceeds amongst the items of equipment, that which embodies superior technique to-day, falling gradually back into the position of the most inferior.

If the process goes on evenly between the two sectors, and full employment is preserved, productive capacity of plant and output per head of labour advance step by step together. The number of man-hours of work in the investment sector required to equip a man in the consumption sector remains constant, and the division of the labour force between the two sectors remains constant.

An even development throughout the system which raises output per head equally for all workers is described as *neutral* technical progress. When output per head is raised by more in the investment than in the commodity sector the progress is said to have a *capital-saving* bias, and when it is more in the commodity sector, a *capital-using* bias.

It is to be observed that it is our 'one-commodity' assumption that makes it possible for us to measure the bias in technical progress. When inventions affect the commodities produced we have no simple measure of output per head or of productive capacity and all discussions of the subject necessarily become somewhat vague.

12. WAGES AND PRICES UNDER COMPETITION

Our last group of exercises was conducted in terms of an economy in which all transactions were made in terms of consumer goods. This is not to be taken literally for it would obviously be impossible to run an economy in which workers are employed for wages on that basis unless it really was a one-commodity world, so that each employer could pay his workers out of their own product.

We must postulate that in our model of a capitalist economy wages are paid in money tokens which are generally acceptable so that they have purchasing power over whatever is available to purchase.

How are the money prices of commodities determined? There are infinite complications involved in the answer to this question, for the policy of the firms may be of many different kinds, and the action of each firm affects the position of others. This question is discussed in Part Four. Here we shall cut through the tangle by taking as the standard case one in which commodities are sold under competitive conditions. Firms may be enlarging their capacity by investing in new plants, but at any moment certain plants exist, and, to make things simple for ourselves, we have assumed that each plant has a well defined capacity output. By competitive conditions, in the short-period sense, we mean that firms endeavour to set prices at

D

the level that will enable them to operate their existing plants at full capacity. (We must except from this rule conditions of a buyer's market, which will be discussed later.) This means that when demand is running ahead of supply, so that stocks in the shops are running down and orders are passed back to the plants for a higher rate of output than that which can be provided with existing capacity, prices are raised so as to choke back demand, and in the reverse position (provided it does not go so deep as to create a buyer's market) prices are lowered so as to stimulate demand sufficiently to permit capacity output to be sold. On this basis we can set out a neat and simple analysis of the determination of prices.

At capacity there is a certain rate of output of commodities and a certain amount of employment in the commodity sector. The level of prices has to be such that the total flow of expenditure coming from households will serve to purchase that rate of output of commodities.

The volume of expenditure over any period, on our assumptions, is equal to the wage bill of that period, plus the outlay of rentiers. Given the money-wage rate (which we assume to be uniform for all labour) the wage bill is determined by the amount of employment. Employment can be divided into that offered by plants producing commodities and that which is concerned with investment in means of production. The outlay of the wage bill of the commodity sector covers itself. The outlay of the wages of workers engaged in investment provides a surplus of receipts over wages costs in the sale of commodities and a further surplus is provided by the expenditure of rentiers. The surplus per unit of output is the *gross margin* on sales.

Figure 12

This can be illustrated as follows. Take employment on the x axis and money per week on the y axis. Mark OC as employment in the commodity sector and CI as employment in the investment sector. OW' (on the y axis) is the money wage per man per week. Draw a perpendicular to the y axis at W' (the wage line) to cut the perpendicular at C in W. Then the wage bill is $CW.OI$ or $CW.OC+CW.CI$. Draw a rectangular hyperbola with asymptotes in the y axis and the wage line, subtending an area equal to $CW.CI$. Let the hyperbola cut CW produced in i. Then Wi is the surplus per man employed in the commodity sector that can be accounted for by the expenditure of wages earned in the investment sector. Now add another curve above the last such that at every point the area of the rectangle made by its vertical distance above the last curve and its lateral distance from the y axis is equal to the weekly outlay of rentiers. Let this curve cut CW produced in p. Then ip is the contribution to surplus per man employed in the commodity sector that can be accounted for by the expenditure of rentiers. Cp is the sales value of the average week's output of a man employed in the commodity sector and Wp is the gross margin on that amount of output. Since physical output is given by technical conditions, this determines the level of selling prices of commodities when the capacity output is being sold.

The competitive level of prices (corresponding to Cp in the diagram) is that which allows full-capacity output to be sold. If prices were set higher than this there would be less employment in the commodity sector. The total profit would not be affected (assuming that investment is unaffected and that unemployed workers have nothing to spend), for the higher profit margin would be offset by reduced sales. If prices were set lower than the full-capacity level, there would be an excess of demand over supply (which might show itself in stocks running down or in queues and shortages in the shops).

All this closely resembles the analysis of the price system in a socialist economy (Part One §13). This is because we have postulated competitive conditions which produce the same result—full-capacity working —as our planners were aiming at.

13. RENTIER INCOME AND EXPENDITURE

So far we have taken the expenditure of rentiers as an arbitrary datum. This is quite reasonable for short-period analysis, for the rentiers, being people of property, are not confined in their expenditure by their receipts; they have wealth and borrowing power which enable them to dissave if they want to. On the other hand, the very fact that they are rentiers shows that they or their ancestors were in the habit of saving. They are free to spend more than their receipts in any period but they normally spend less.

For many problems it is reasonable and convenient to assume that the rentiers' expenditure is a definite proportion of their receipts (there are some tricky questions involved when they are expecting their receipts to be at a different rate in the future from what they have been in the immediate past, but we need not go into that at the moment).

The rentiers' receipts consist of payments of interest on bonds and dividends on shares. The amount of interest on bonds owed by firms depends very largely on historical accident—how much the firms happened to have been financed in that way and what rate of interest was ruling at the time. The amount of dividends paid is partly a matter of competition between firms. Each one (on the reading of their psychology that we have chosen to follow) would prefer to keep as much profit as possible to finance its own growth, but it is obliged to pay about the same proportion of profits out in dividends as others do, or it will not be able to borrow on shares again, and may even be attacked by its shareholders, who are its legal owners, after all. Thus the pressure of competition keeps them more or less in line with each other, but the level established for all taken together is rather arbitrary.

The sums paid out by the firms to rentiers, less the amounts saved, return to them as receipts and swell their profits. The total profit of the firms is equal to the expenditure of rentiers plus the wages bill for the investment sector, which together make up the profit on sale of commodities, plus the profits of the invest-ment sector (which may be a mere book entry when the firm itself owns the machine-making plants which provide it with new equipment). The excess of profits over investment depends upon the rentiers expenditure (for we are assuming that wages are in any case fully spent). The saving of the rentiers, in any period, is the excess of their receipts over their expenditure, and this is equal to the excess of the expenditure of the firms, taken as a whole, over their receipts, that is, their bor-rowing from the rentiers. The excess of the value of the investments made by the firms, taken as a whole, over their borrowing is the same thing as their retained profits. These relations can be set out in a simple formula:

P = total profits of a period
I = value of investment of the period
d = proportion of profits distributed
s = proportion of rentiers' receipts saved

Then $I = (1 - d + sd) P$

$$P = I \frac{1}{(1 - d) + sd}$$

For example, if we put I as 100, d as 70 per cent and s as $\frac{1}{7}$, then total profits are $100 \big/ \left(\frac{3}{10} + \frac{1}{10} \right) = 250$. Of this rentiers receive 175 and save 25. The firms retain 75. Of the 100 of investment, 75 has been financed out of retained profits and 25 has been borrowed from rentiers.

In itself, this is merely book-keeping, but if in reality the ratios d and s are given by the behaviour of firms and rentiers in a fairly regular manner over reasonably long periods of time, the analysis takes on a more than formal meaning, for it shows how the level of profits adapts itself to the given conditions in such a way as to bring the level of savings, as determined by these habits, into line with the level of outlay on investment.

This is an alternative version of the famous proposition that savings are equal to investment. In its original form it was concerned with the level of employment. Here we are seeing how the equalisation of savings with investment works out through the level of profits, whether employment is affected or not.

Borrowing by firms from rentiers may take place directly by the sale of securities to them, or it may take place through banks, which accept deposits from rentiers and lend to firms. We are not proposing to offer any exercises on monetary problems. We shall merely postulate that a sufficient amount of finance is supplied through the banking system to provide an adequate amount of acceptable means of payment and to satisfy any desire to hoard cash that rentiers may feel, so that the needs of the active circulation are always provided for without any strain.

14. OBSOLESCENCE AND AMORTISATION

To maintain their productive capacity, firms have to retain a sufficient allowance, from the earnings of a plant, to replace it when it ceases to earn. When technical progress is going on, its length of serviceable life does not depend only on physical durability.

At any moment the most progressive firms have recently installed the newest techniques, superior to those used by their rivals. At given money prices they can pay somewhat higher money-wage rates, or at given money-wage rates they can sell at somewhat lower prices, and still enjoy higher profits than the firms with old plants, where productivity is less. The pressure of competition enforces lower gross margins upon the old plants, for the progressive firms cut margins in their endeavour to expand their own sales and if the others do not follow suit they will lose labour or lose customers. As time goes by plants embodying ever-superior techniques come into being and consequently the margin on employing labour with any one given plant falls off over its life, as it has to meet competition which grows progressively more severe, until finally it yields no margin at all and is driven out of use. This is similar to the obsolescence due to deepening investment that we met with in Part One §18, v, but it is not the same thing, for in this case there is no deepening taking place and there is no reason why the prospective profits on new investment should be falling off, as does the marginal efficiency of investment when the degree of mechanisation is being raised.

The expectation that obsolescence will occur affects the behaviour of firms in two ways. It means that when they are considering a new investment, taking into account the length of earning life that can be expected from it, they reckon on obsolescence as well as physical wear and tear. And it affects their policy about amortisation on plant which has been installed. The first point we will discuss in a moment. Meanwhile we must consider the second with some care, for it is one of the great mystifications of the capitalist system.

As we saw with our employer in the last section, after a fund of finance has been embodied in physical capital it can become detached from it again and pursue a course of its own as rentier wealth. The original subscribers or lenders can sell their shares or bonds at second hand, and replace the proceeds in some other concern, hoard it as cash, or spend it, thereby dissaving and consuming rentier wealth. Meanwhile the physical capital carries on as before. The physical capital also can be consumed if it is allowed to wear out without being replaced. (It is important to notice the difference between disinvestment, which means taking the proceeds from physical capital without restoring it, and a loss of capital such as occurs when, for instance, there is an unforeseen fall of demand. In the latter case it has become impossible to extract the finance originally embodied in the capital out of its earnings, for it is the earning power of the capital which has evaporated.)

Now, we are postulating that the firms in our model are not spivs, who make a quick profit and quit, but are imbued with a high sense of duty. They regard it as morally wrong to consume capital in either sense. They wish at least to preserve (and usually to increase) both the amount of rentier wealth that their capital comprises and its physical productive capacity. They may not always be able to do so, for some fall by the way in the competitive struggle, but in any case they go down fighting.

The two duties are interconnected. When finance has been borrowed from outside and invested in a plant of limited earning life, then either the debt must be repaid during the life of the plant so that a fresh loan can be taken to replace it, or the debt remains outstanding and a fund must have been built up to replace the plant with a fresh one to earn the interest on the debt. Equally if the firm operates with its own funds it cannot continue in existence unless the earnings of its plants provide the finance for their own replacement.

At the same time there is no close relationship in detail between maintaining capital in its physical aspect and its financial aspect. Generally plants do not have a simple life span. Particular parts wear out or grow obsolete faster than others, so that a continual process of piecemeal renewal is always going on. Most parts (and all whole plants) are replaced by something different from themselves, embodying newer, superior techniques, so that an exact distinction between replacement and expansion of productive capacity is meaningless.

From the wealth point of view it is perfectly legitimate to recover finance from the earnings of a plant and use the proceeds to make loans. It would be a violation of the second duty (to preserve productive capacity) for a firm thus to turn itself from a productive enterprise into a purely financial one, but for a spell of time there is no objection to holding finance uninvested, waiting for a favourable moment to commit it once more to physical capital.

Thus the relation between a firm's capital from the physical and the financial points of view is quite loose, and there is no absolutely clear and obvious relationship between the amortisation of a particular portion of finance and a particular piece of physical capital, even if its future earning life could be foreseen with certainty. On top of this, the future is never certain and earning life is always a matter of guesswork.

To be on the safe side, the proper procedure for a firm is, on the one hand, to endeavour to keep its total productive capacity expanding in whatever appears to be the best available form, for in doing so it will automatically replace (and more than replace) any physical capital being scrapped; on the other hand, to set amortisation charges against its earnings so as to write off the book value of all investments over a rather shorter time than it hopes the earning life of the physical capital will actually be. In doing so it automatically prevents itself from treating as income and distributing so much of its earnings as to reduce the financial value of its capital.

Figure 12—continued

To illustrate, complete the last diagram by adding two notional cost curves, one to represent the week's share in the amortisation charge which the firms feel it proper to allow on the plant, and the other the week's share of the sums which they are distributing to rentiers—each averaged out over the distance OC (which represents employment) in the same way as the outlay of rentiers and the investment wages bill. Let the upper of the two notional cost curves cut CW produced in t. Then Ct is the total cost per man employed from the point of view of the firms selling commodities. If t lies above p they are failing to recover what they regard as a proper rate of amortisation, and (taken collectively) they are losing financial capital.

An excess of notional total costs over receipts (t above p in the diagram) would not occur in normal conditions. The reaction of firms to such a situation will be discussed later. When total receipts from the sale of commodities exceed notional costs (p lies above t) they are gaining financial capital and part of the new physical capital that is being created will belong to them without any debt attached. When total receipts are just covering the outgoings of the firms *plus* amortisation (t and p coincide) they are just maintaining the financial value of their capital. In so far as amortisation allowances have been set at an unnecessarily generous level, the firms are doing more net saving of their own than they allow themselves to believe, and in so far as they are too low, the firms are losing financial capital without knowing it.

15. THE CHOICE OF TECHNIQUE BY A FIRM

When a firm has finance to invest, whether newly borrowed or forthcoming from its own funds, whether replacing old capacity or creating new, it has to settle the question of the form that the investment is to take. The amount of finance to be invested at any one time may be limited by its borrowing power or by desire to go step by step and digest one investment before embarking on another. Whatever the amount, the form will be chosen from amongst the technical possibilities open at the moment so as to use the finance to the best · advantage.

The investment which the firm is planning is only a small part of the whole economy and, in normal conditions, it regards itself as free to recruit as much or as little labour as it pleases. The cost of employing labour is governed by the ruling wage rate. The choice of the form of investment therefore somewhat resembles that of the socialist economy before full employment has been reached (Part One §17) but it differs in that the firm reckons entirely in money terms, that it is in a less good position to predict the future behaviour of the economy, and that it follows what it holds to be its patriotic duty to itself, not to society as a whole. The duty of the firm is to choose the form of investment that promises the highest profit on the finance to be invested, for it is profit that supplies the ammunition for its constant struggle to survive and expand.

To simplify the argument we will suppose that the investment is to be in a complete plant. The cost of a plant (eliminating as usual transactions in materials, etc.) is the wages paid to the investment workers who build it, *plus* the profit margin which constitutes the earnings of the plant in which they work, and *plus* an allowance for the cost of waiting over its gestation period. The latter is not measured by the rate of interest that happens to be charged on the finance being expended, but rather by the rate of profit that could be earned if the finance were used to acquire capital which is already yielding a profit.

We imagine the firm to compare, on paper, plants embodying various techniques all having the same cost when reckoned in this way. We assume that the finance to be invested is sufficient to acquire a plant, of whatever technique, large enough to enjoy all the relevant economies of scale.

It very much simplifies the exercise if we assume that all plants are expected to have about the same earning life and each to be workable at a constant level of efficiency over its life. We can then compare their relative profitability simply on the basis of the profit margins that they will yield, without having to bother about amortisation.

Now, if there is one technique which is superior to the rest in the sense that an investment of the given amount of finance in a plant of that type yields a higher rate of output while requiring a smaller amount of labour to operate it, there is no problem—that is the technique to choose.

Where there are several techniques of different degrees of mechanisation, all at the same level (that is, none inferior to any other), the plant which employs less labour has a smaller ouptut.

Figure 13

The choice of the most profitable technique can be illustrated by an adaptation of the diagram which we used for the socialist economy.

Take on the x axis labour employed per week in a plant of the given cost. On the y axis take expected money proceeds per week. Since the expected price of the product is not affected by the type of plant (in competitive conditions) this is equivalent to taking the rate of output. Mark the points α, β, and γ showing employment and output for plants belonging to three techniques in descending order of degree of mechanisation. α lies southwest of β (that is, below and to the left). The Alpha technique is more mechanised than Beta, requiring less labour and offering less output. γ lies to the northeast of β. The slope of the line $\alpha\beta$ is steeper than of $\beta\gamma$.

Now draw a straight line from the origin rising to the right to represent the wage bill. The slope of this line is the wage per man per week. The height of the points α, β and γ above the wage line represents the excess of proceeds over wages costs per week with each type of plant. The eligible technique is that for which this distance is the greatest.

It is the cost of labour in terms of its own product which governs the relative profitability of techniques from the point of view of the firm. The advantage of a more mechanised technique in economising labour per unit of output is more important the higher the wage rate.

Figure 13—continued

To compare positions with different money-wage rates and the same price of product, superimpose on the last diagram a higher wage line. (The cost of the investment has been readjusted to provide for a higher money cost of capital goods with the same productivity.) It can immediately be seen that the balance of advantage has shifted to a more mechanised technique.

Similarly, a higher money price of the product with the same wage rate can be shown by raising the points α, β and γ in the same proportion. The advantage then tilts towards a less mechanised technique.

Our notation can be extended to deal with movements through time, *plus* signs being used to denote superior techniques, and the Greek letters to denote the degree of mechanisation.

When technical progress is going on, possible superior techniques may be discovered over the whole range of degrees of mechanisation. The physical form of equipment may be completely changed but we can identify the degree of mechanisation by the rate of profit on investment at which the technique is eligible. Thus if a new technique superior to Beta has come into existence which would be chosen if the new level of real wages were such as to make the rate of profit on investment the same as it was when Beta was chosen, we can reckon it as being of the Beta degree of mechanisation and call it Beta-plus. Similarly, we can distinguish Gamma-plus, Alpha-plus, Beta-double-plus, and so forth.

When technical progress is neutral the value in terms of commodities of investment per unit of output is the same for Beta and for Beta-plus technique, for Beta-plus is chosen when the real wage rate has risen in the same ratio as output per head, and since output per head has risen equally in both sectors, the cost of investment per man employed has risen in the same ratio as the real wage rate.

It should not be necessary to repeat the warning that our highly simplified exercise is only scratching the surface of some very deep questions.

16. MARGINAL PRODUCTS ONCE MORE

For each adjacent pair of techniques there is a cost of labour in terms of product that makes them equally eligible, and when the gradation of techniques is very fine a different pair becomes eligible for each small change in the cost of labour.

Figure 13—continued

Thus, in the diagram, it can be seen that if the slope of the wage line happened to be the same as that of $\alpha\beta$, Alpha and Beta techniques are equally eligible, or if it is the same as $\beta\gamma$, Gamma and Beta are equally eligible.

If there is such a fine gradation of techniques that two are equally eligible at every wage rate, $\alpha\beta\gamma$ becomes a continuous curve. Then, whatever the slope of the wage line there is a tangent parallel to it at some point or other on the curve, indicating two adjacent points at the same height above the wage line.

It may be noted that the slope of such a tangent in the diagram indicates the marginal product of labour from the point of view of the firm, for here we have a given quantity of investment of finance, employing two slightly different quantities of labour. The additional output produced by the slightly less mechanised technique, divided by the additional labour employed, is the marginal product of labour from the point of view of the firm, and this, as we see, is equal to the wage rate at which this pair of techniques is eligible. Thus we can turn the proposition round and say that, granted that the firm is going to make a certain investment of finance, then in order to get the maximum possible return from the investment it must plan to employ with it such a number of workers as will make the marginal product of labour from the firm's point of view equal to the wage. And we can express the influence of the wage rate on the choice of technique by saying that the level of wages induces the firm to choose a technique such that the marginal product of labour from its point of view is equal to the wage.

If we take it that the whole plant is going to be an addition to the productive capacity of the firm and the workers employed in it an addition to the firm's labour force, then we can say that the total proceeds from the additional capacity, *minus* the profit margin which covers amortisation and profit on the capital invested, is expected to be equal to the wage bill, so that the marginal *net* product of labour is equal to the wage. This is perfectly correct but not very interesting.

17. THE PROFITABILITY OF INVESTMENT

So far we have been considering the choice between various possible forms that a given investment might take. We must now consider the prospective profitability of investment, assuming that the most eligible form is always chosen.

According to the code of behaviour of the firms in our model, any investment once made is intended to be permanent, but plants, or items in a plant, when they come to the end of their earning life are not generally replaced with replicas of themselves. They are required to have contributed, before they die, the equivalent of a replacement, taking whatever form is most eligible at the time when it is made. The investment is intended to be immortal though the plant is not.

The profitability of an investment from the point of view of the firm that makes it can be expressed, analogously to the marginal efficiency of investment from the point of view of the economy as a whole (see Part One §18, iii), as the rate of discount which reduces the series of expected future earnings of the capital concerned to equality with its initial cost. This concept involves all those difficulties which we met with in connection with marginal efficiency, and cannot take much weight except in cases where the rate of profit, so conceived, is confidently expected to remain constant over the indefinite future.

In our one-commodity world, where the distribution of income between families has no effect upon the composition of output, with competition functioning freely, in tranquil conditions which make the future fairly predictable, and when absolutely full employment of labour prevails, the profitability of investment from the point of view of firms is equivalent to the marginal efficiency of investment from the point of view of the economy as a whole. (This matter is further discussed in Part Five.)

18. A GOLDEN AGE

After these preliminaries we can set the model of a capitalist economy to work. We shall proceed by first examining an economy which is developing in a smooth and harmonious manner; next we compare different economies each on a smooth path; then we discuss how an economy behaves when there is a lack of harmony between particular elements in it; finally we examine the reaction of an economy travelling on a rough path and encountering shocks which throw it out of equilibrium.

At first we consider an economy with its productive capacity being fully utilised, with full employment, constant prices, a constant rate of profit on investment expected, and expectations in fact being realised, the whole expanding with all its parts in proportion at a steady exponential rate—so much per cent. per annum cumulatively. I have called this a *golden age* to emphasise its mythical character.

The existence and continuance of such a state of affairs requires certain technical conditions and certain patterns of behaviour which may be listed as follows:

(i) The plant in existence offers employment to all available labour when it is operated at capacity.

(ii) The level of prices in relation to money incomes and saving habits is such as to keep the commodity sector working at capacity.

(iii) The eagerness of firms to invest, their willingness to take risks and their command of finance are such as to keep the investment sector working to capacity.

(iv) The gestation period of plant remains constant, so that the level of output of new productive capacity ready to use does not vary relatively to the rate of investment. In so far as it is the physical length of life of plant which limits its earning life, the length of life remains constant, so that with a steadily growing rate of output of new plant there is a steady exponential rate of growth of the total stock in existence, measured in terms of productive capacity.

(v) There is a harmonious relation between the level of real wages ruling and the degree of mechanisation of the technique in use, so that no firm is under an incentive to change its plant over to a higher or lower degree—when the degree of mechanisation ruling is Beta, no one is wanting to replace Beta with Alpha or Gamma plant. New superior techniques chosen are at the same degree of mechanisation, so that the system is evolving from Beta to Beta-plus to Beta-double-plus, etc. When potential physical life is longer than earning life, the rate of obsolescence is such as to give a constant earning life to plant. These conditions dictate a certain rate of increase of productive capacity.

(vi) The relation of the capacity of the two sectors is such as to permit this rate of growth of capacity to be maintained.

(vii) The golden age can be realised only if labour to man the plant is forthcoming. Output at full employment of the labour force must be expanding at the same rate as output at full capacity of plant. This condition is fulfilled when technical progress is neutral, going on at a steady rate, so that output per head is growing at a steady rate which is uniform throughout the economy, and the labour force is growing in numbers at a steady rate (which may be zero), hours of work per man-year being constant. The combination of growing numbers with growing output per head keeps the full employment rate of output in each sector expanding at the same rate as productive capacity. This rate of growth is the *growth ratio* of the golden-age economy.

(viii) To maintain an expansion of output at the growth ratio it is necessary that money expenditure on commodities should be growing with productive capacity.

(a) This requires the money wage bill to be growing at the growth rate. In so far as the labour force is growing, the wage bill grows proportionately, and in so far as output per head is growing the money wage rate must rise at the same rate. (We are assuming that wages are fully spent currently as they are received.)

(b) Retained profits remain at a constant proportion of profits, and the propensity of rentier families to save remains constant (the d and s of our formula in §13 remain constant).

When all these provisos are fulfilled the labour force remains divided in a constant proportion between the sectors, and is fully employed. The price level of commodities is constant. The shares of the two classes of families in total income remain constant. The rate of profit on investment remains constant. These are the characteristics of a golden age.

19. COMPARISON OF GOLDEN AGES

Within reason, any combination of technical conditions and savings habits of families has its appropriate golden age. Taking the above Beta golden age as a basis and comparing with it another economy which has just reached the same phase of technical development, so that the latest, most superior, techniques are the same in both, we may say that, if the growth ratio in the latter is greater, while the propensity to save out of profits is the same (d and s the same), then, if golden age conditions are realised, the proportion of the labour force in the investment sector is greater and the real wage rate lower.

Since the cost of labour, in terms of their own product, to the firms is lower in the economy with the higher rate of growth, the degree of mechanisation is less (except in some very cranky cases). At the stage of development at which the Beta economy is using Beta technique the faster-growing one is using Gamma technique. The Beta-plus stage in the former corresponds to Gamma-plus in the latter, and so forth. The rate of profit on investment is higher in the Gamma economy, for the lower real wage rate means that even if Beta technique were used, profits would be higher, while Gamma is actually preferred because at the real wage rate ruling it yields a higher rate of return than Beta.

With the higher rate of profit, there is a greater preference in the Gamma economy for quick-yielding investments, but, on the other hand, the working life of a given type of plant tends to be longer.

Similarly, we can work out comparisons of potential golden ages with the same growth ratio and different propensities to save—a lower propensity to save out of profits being associated with a lower real wage and a lower degree of mechanisation.

The only limitation that we must set upon the range of possibilities is that the growth ratio must not be so high and the propensity to save so low as to cause real wages to be less than the level which is considered tolerable in the community concerned.

The condition for realising a potential golden age is that the firms should carry out the requisite rate of investment.

20. AN ALTERNATIVE FORMULATION

Another way of setting out the comparison of golden ages is in terms of the value of capital and the rate of profit on capital. Each golden age, having existed for a long past in perfectly harmonious conditions with a constant rate of profit on investment, possesses a stock of capital the value of which is the sum of all net investments made in the past, and the rate of profit on capital (which always has been and is expected to remain constant) is equal to the rate of profit on investment.

On this basis we may say that in the Gamma economy, with a higher growth ratio and the same propensity to save as the Beta economy, in golden-age conditions, the ratio of the value of net investment to the value of the stock of capital is greater and the rate of profit higher. The ratio of saving to value of capital is correspondingly higher, for profit per unit of capital is greater and savings are proportional to profits.

It is impossible to say whether saving per unit of income is greater or less, for while profit per unit of capital is higher in Gamma, income per unit of capital is also higher. By the same token, we cannot say anything about the share of wages in income, for while the wage per man is less at a given stage of technical development, so is the value of output per man. (The case where the relative shares of wages and profits are the same at different degrees of mechanisation is sometimes described as 'unit elasticity of substitution between labour and capital'.)

We cannot state definitely that the capital/labour ratio in Gamma is less than in Beta for a rather subtle reason. On the one hand, Gamma technique requires a smaller expenditure of investment-sector labour time to equip a man, and the wage rate is lower, but on the other hand, the cost of waiting is higher in the Gamma economy, where the rate of profit is higher, so that it is possible for the Gamma equipment to represent a greater cost of investment than the Beta equipment, per man employed.

This way of looking at things is useful as a check, but it has the serious drawback that it makes no sense outside the setting of a golden age; when we consider an economy which has been following a bumpy path in the past and is looking into an uncertain future, the meaning of the value of the stock of capital and of the rate of profit on capital becomes extremely hazy. It is better, on the whole, to formulate our exercises without resort to these concepts.

21. ANIMAL SPIRITS

The difference between potential golden ages may arise from technical conditions; say, in one the scientists make discoveries that can be put to industrial use at a faster rate, and, perhaps, the population is growing at a faster rate. Or it may be that the difference arises in the first place from a difference in the behaviour of firms. In one they are more eager to accumulate, take a more optimistic attitude to risk (or risks may actually be less, because of better preservation of good order, laws adapted to the convenience of firms, etc.), find rentiers more willing to lend finance so that interest rates are lower, pursue a more aggressive policy in competition amongst themselves, and are more eager to seek out new techniques so that their desire to accumulate causes technical progress to speed up. It is impossible to draw a hard and fast line between conditions external to the firms which govern the potential growth ratio and the energy with which the firms themselves struggle to expand. All we can say is that, for golden age conditions to prevail, it is necessary that both the firms, taken as a whole, should keep up a rate of accumulation not less than is appropriate to the growth ratio, and that the growth ratio should be sufficient to absorb the rate of accumulation that the firms keep up.

When a steady rate of growth is being realised the rate of profit on investment accommodates itself to it; with a given share of rentier consumption, the real wage rate is lower (at a given state of technical development) the greater the proportion of the labour force in the investment sector.

A higher rate of profit is the consequence, not the cause, of greater activity by the firms.

We assume that any rate of profit, within reason, will serve to keep investment going when the firms are used to it, but that a fall in the rate of profit on investment below what it has been in the past is discouraging to them, and that a revival after it has fallen gives them renewed life.

22. ABSTINENCE AND SAVING

We discussed the cost of investment in terms of consumption goods forgone in the family and the socialist economy. This way of looking at things cannot be applied in any simple manner to the capitalist economy, for the distribution of the burden of abstinence between workers and rentier families varies with the ratio of investment to total consumption and with the propensity to consume of the rentiers. At a given level of technical development a larger number of workers in the investment sector entails a smaller output of commodities, and a lower real wage rate. At the same time it entails a higher level of profits and (d and s being given) a higher level of rentier consumption. Thus the workers have to support abstinence not only to match investment but some extra as well to match the higher consumption of rentiers.

The greater is the propensity of rentiers to save (given the rate of investment that is being carried out), the lower is this additional burden of abstinence on the workers. The greater the saving by rentiers, the higher the level of real wages and the lower the level of profits.

Thus thriftiness of rentiers is a benefit to the workers and a drawback to the firms. The firms would prefer (within certain limits) rentiers to spend all they receive, so that the whole investment would be matched by undistributed profits and the firms would not have to incur debts by borrowing finance from rentiers.

The limit to the application of this proposition is that it does not suit the firms for real wages to be pushed below the level considered tolerable, for when that happens money wages have to be raised. This either eats into profits, if prices are not raised correspondingly, or creates an explosive inflation if they are. When the animal spirits of the firms are strong enough to be continually bringing them up against the *inflation barrier* to higher investment set by the tolerable minimum of real wages, they welcome thriftiness of rentiers that pushes the barrier further out and permits a higher rate of investment at any given level of real wages.

23. DISHARMONIES

The conception of a golden age is merely a device to enable us to distinguish the conditions necessary for harmonious development. We now turn to the situation in an economy when various elements are not in the harmonious relations required by a golden age.

The sub-sections are numbered to correspond to the list of characteristics of a golden age in §39.

(i) *Employment and capacity*

(*a*) *Excess labour*. An economy may find itself in a situation when available labour exceeds the employment offered by plant in existence. To a mild extent this is normal in capitalist economies; absolutely full employment is very rare and when it does occur it is usually accompanied by over-capacity working of plant. When the condition of excess labour is of serious dimensions it is known as chronic or non-Keynesian unemployment, for it cannot be remedied merely by increasing effective demand. We shall refer to it as non-employment, using the term unemployment for the case where workers have had jobs in the past and have now lost them. If the labour force is growing faster than the stock of productive capacity there is a growth of non-employment, the situation getting progressively worse as time goes by.

There are three kinds of reaction that are helpful in this situation. The one is to speed up investment (if necessary working investment-sector plant above normal capacity for a time until the stock of it has been increased). This in itself increases employment while the investment is going on and, by causing productive capacity to increase at a faster rate, contributes gradually to reducing permanent non-employment. (If at the same time technical progress can be given a capital-saving bias so much the better. This involves seeking out superior techniques requiring little invest-ment per man employed, so that a given rate of investment increases employment faster.) This is what we should expect in a socialist economy, but there is no particular reason why capitalist firms should react in this way. They may be carrying on a rate of accumulation which is quite adequate from their own point of view and enjoying satisfactory profits. They find the existence of a large reserve of labour very convenient from many points of view. The age may look quite sufficiently golden to them, in spite of the growing misery of workers' families.

Another reaction is to set about lowering the degree of mechanisation, replacing Beta plant with Gamma (or with Gamma-plus, in so far as technical progress is taking place during the time that de-mechanisation is going on). There is a certain tendency for this to happen. Money wage rates may be cut by the competition of workers eager for jobs, and in any case they are not likely to rise in step with technical progress, while competition may not be strong enough immediately to push prices down to the corresponding extent, so that prices drift above the capacity level. The effect is to reduce output below capacity (this is another disharmony which we shall discuss in a moment) so that employment not only fails to increase to catch up on the available labour, but actually declines. The situation is now one in which the cost of labour from the point of view of the firms (the wage in terms of product) has fallen. A less mechanised technique than that in use has become eligible and the investment which is going on can be switched to producing a type of plant that will require more labour to operate it. In so far as this happens it helps gradually to reduce the numbers of potential workers not employed and to increase total output. It cannot be relied upon, however; switching technique to take advantage of a different real-wage rate is just as troublesome to firms as investing in superior techniques and, since the original disharmony arose from firms being too slack to keep up with the potential growth ratio of the economy, it would be rather strange if they were very eager and active in adjusting the degree of mechanisation.

The third helpful reaction comes into play if the rentier families feel a concern for the families of the non-employed and arrange some kind of *dole* payment which does not reduce their own consumption by as much as it increases that of the workers. Then total demand for commodities goes up with the total population and their prices, at capacity output, rise as time goes by. In the first instance this is a burden upon the workers already employed, for real wages are reduced, but in so far as there is any short-period elasticity of supply, output from given plant will be increased and the higher level of profits may stimulate firms to increase productive capacity and so help partially to remove the basic trouble.

(b) *Excess plant.* Disharmony the other way round— a deficiency of labour relatively to plant in existence—is less liable to occur, for firms will not wittingly build plant that cannot be manned. However, it is not an impossible situation, and we must examine it.

Capacity is not now the bottle-neck and some or all plants are working under capacity for lack of hands. Profits are below the golden age level, but the short-period marginal product of labour is high and firms are eager to get more workers. Money wages are bid up. Prices rise, as a result of the additional expenditure of the workers' families, but they do not rise fully in proportion to wage rates, because the rentiers' receipts have not gone up, and we may assume that their expenditure rises, if at all, in a smaller proportion than prices.

With a scarcity of labour and higher real wages the firms set about increasing the degree of mechanisation to raise output per head. They may also be spurred to speed up the introduction of superior techniques, so that old plant is scrapped sooner than it would normally have been and new plant, fitted to the available labour with a higher rate of output, takes its place.

After passing through a period of turbulence the firms get plant into adjustment to available labour and (if no other disharmony exists) slip into the path of golden-age development.

(ii) *The degree of monopoly*. In the golden age the level of prices of commodities is such as to ensure the steady rate of sale of the capacity output of plants. Prices may be set higher than this level. Firms taken as a whole cannot make any more total gross profit on a week's sales than the outlay of the investment-sector workers and of rentiers; but firms do not operate as a whole; particular groups of firms may believe that they can do better by charging prices higher than the golden-age level. On the assumptions of our model, some will in fact do better, for we assume that families buy baskets of goods made up in a particular way, and if they have to pay more for one item they have less to spend on others; if the prices of some items are kept up by monopolistic agreements, the prices of others sold under fully competitive conditions will be so much the lower. Thus while the total of profit remains the same, the groups of firms which can agree to restrict competition and keep up prices get a greater share of it. When some do so, others follow, for if they do not they suffer a loss of profits.

When prices in general are controlled in this way, so that the total cost of a basket of goods is above the competitive level (given money wage rates), it is impossible to sell the full capacity output.

Figure 12—continued

This can be easily seen on the short-period diagram. Enter a price line above Cp. The point where it cuts the p curve indicates the amount of employment in the commodity sector that will be compatible with that level of prices.

The above is somewhat too simple, for it is not reasonable to assume that the money expenditure of rentiers is independent of the level of prices. At higher prices they may spend a larger proportion of their money receipts (their savings habits being dependent upon real rather than money income). Allowing for the effects of this, however, it remains true that higher prices relatively to money wages mean a lower rate of sale of commodities, for though in the extreme case the rentiers buy no less than they would have done at lower prices, the workers cannot do so, and total purchases are necessarily reduced.

The same situation may come about through a different attitude on the part of firms. They may eschew monopolistic agreements or understandings to keep up prices, but they may believe that it is right and proper to charge prices which cover their full costs, and the notional element in costs may be set too high to permit them to be covered.

Figure 12—continued

In the diagram, illustrate a case where the t curve lies above the p curve. There is now no feasible combination of price and output that covers the costs shown on the t curve.

If firms, in such a situation, tried to fix prices to cover costs they would produce a disastrously low level of output. We may assume that the firms in our model have more sense than this, but they may have established a convention that prices ought to be such that, if full capacity output *were* sold at those prices, full costs would be covered. That is to say, they charge prices equal to notional average cost (Ct in the diagram) and sell whatever output is saleable at that level of prices.

Whatever the reason that keeps prices above the full capacity level, the situation may be permanent if the extent of surplus capacity is small, but if it is large and expected to remain so, then investment is discouraged (for there is no point in maintaining capacity that will never be used) and the economy will pass through a period of stagnation with low investment and unemployment until the surplus capacity has been disposed of. In the long run, therefore, monopoly shows itself in a smaller amount of capacity rather than an under-utilisation of what capacity there is.

(iii) *The rate of investment*

(a) *Stagnation*. When the firms are slack and are not keeping up with the potential growth ratio of the economy, the level of activity is falling progressively further and further below the full employment mark. In so far as the labour force is growing in numbers, the growing reserve of non-employed labour may be popularly attributed to over-population; and in so far as output per head is growing faster than output, the consequent discharge of redundant workers is popularly described as 'technological unemployment'; in either case the basic trouble is the same—too low a rate of accumulation of productive capacity.

The reason for the slackness of firms may be that risks are too great, that finance is hard to come by or that they have relaxed the competitive struggle and are pursuing a policy of live and let live amongst themselves.

If we remove the assumption of a given quantum of work per employed worker, we may envisage part or all of the under-employment in a stagnant economy being absorbed by shorter hours of work, paid holidays, etc., and a shorter working life—longer education and earlier retirement. If stagnation sets in when the level of consumption in terms of commodities is fairly high, it can offer quite a comfortable life to all concerned.

(b) *Ebullience.* In the opposite case the eagerness of firms to invest is such that they are accumulating productive capacity at a rate faster than the growth ratio. (We recognised that the growth ratio itself partly depends upon the activity of firms; in the case we are now considering they are carrying out accumulation even faster than the rate to which they have succeeded in pushing up the growth ratio.)

The only way that more accumulation can be accommodated is by increasing the degree of mechanisation. Thus this economy must be moving from Beta to Alpha-plus technique while the corresponding golden-age path runs from Beta to Beta-plus. How can this come about? The proportion of the labour force in the investment sector is greater than in the golden-age economy and (assuming the same propensity to save of rentiers) the rate of profit on investment is consequently greater and the real wage rate lower. In equilibrium conditions this would entail a lower degree of mechanisation. We seem to have landed ourselves in a contradiction. The answer is that in their eagerness to expand the firms are continually on the brink of creating the situation, discussed above, where the capacity of plant is too great for the available labour force. They can see it coming (or a few go over the brink and others are warned) and so set about deflecting investment to Alpha-plus plant in spite of the fact that, if labour were freely available at the ruling real wage rate, Gamma-plus would be more eligible.

Now with a given rate of investment ruling there is a given selling value of output per man in the commodity sector, while the cost of the newest equipment for a man employed in the commodity sector has risen with the substitution of Alpha-plus for Beta technique. The rate of profit on investment has therefore fallen.

We are assuming that, although a golden age may be possible at any level of profits, once established, yet a fall in the rate of profit below what it has been in the recent past has a damping effect on the enthusiasm of the firms for investment. It may tend also to make finance harder to come by. So long as they persist in increasing the degree of mechanisation they continue to depress the rate of profit on investment. (This is analogous to the fall in marginal efficiency of investment that we observed in the socialist economy which was deepening productive capacity.)

We cannot, therefore, imagine this process going on for long. Sooner or later the exuberance of the firms will flag and they will sink back to the growth ratio. Indeed there is no reason to suppose that this kind of 'deepening' investment ever occurs in capitalist economies. (We must not be deceived into thinking that great masses of elaborate machinery generally indicate a high degree of mechanisation. They are far more likely to indicate highly superior techniques.)

(iv) *The stock of plant.* The stock of plant in existence at any moment reflects the history of investment and scrapping over a fairly long past, just as the age composition of a population reflects past birth and death rates.

When investment has been subject to fits and starts or the durability of plant has varied from one round of investment to another, or the gestation period has varied, so that a given rate of investment has led to a variable growth of the stock of plant ready for use, the stock of plant in being will be full of irregularities. At

E

one moment a large amount, and at another moment very little, will be falling due to be replaced, so that a steady rate of output of new capacity will give a variable rate of change of the stock in existence. This sets up perturbations in the course of development. It is impossible to be in a golden age without having been in one for a long time.

(v) *Wages and technique.* The economy may find itself in a situation in which the ruling real wage rate is not the one which makes the ruling degree of mechanisation the most eligible. We have already seen how a fall in real wages due to a growth in the reserve of non-employed labour may lead to a de-mechanisation of technique. It might also happen, in the vicissitudes of development, that the wage rate and degree of mechanisation have got out of gear although full employment is being maintained. In such a case it is the real wage rate that will come into line. Suppose that there is full employment with Beta technique, but the wage rate happens to be such as to make Gamma eligible. Some firms switching over to Gamma plants, while intending to keep their output the same, require more hands, and since there was already full employment their attempt to recruit men pushes up wages relatively to prices until Gamma technique ceases to be eligible. Contrariwise, a switch to Alpha technique when there is full employment at Beta creates unemployment and helps to bring wages down to the Beta level.

In the exercise which we considered just now, the firms in an economy whose growth rate was appropriate to a Beta golden age carried out a burst of deepening investment which led them to install Alpha-plus plant. The consequent fall in the rate of profit on investment pulled them back to the golden age rate of accumulation. But they are employing all available labour (workers released by the fall in the rate of investment having been absorbed into the commodity sector) and they cannot now de-mechanise and return to the Beta path. Moreover, the duty which firms have to maintain the value of an investment once made has caused them to set higher amortisation allowances against their plant, so that rentier consumption is relatively reduced. Thus real wages are permanently higher as a result of the passing fit of exuberance of the firms. Conversely, a period of stagnation when a low degree of mechanisation has been adopted leaves a legacy of permanently lower productivity and lower real wages even if the economy later gets into the golden age path.

(vi) *Disproportionalities*. In the vicissitudes of development it may easily happen that the relation between the productive capacity in the two sectors is out of line with the rates of output which the firms wish to produce. There is a strong tendency in the system to correct disproportionalities of this kind; the type of plant which is scarce yields a high rate of profit on investment and that which is redundant a low rate of profit (or none) so that the firms direct investment in such a way as to bring the stock of plant into balance. There is very likely, however, to be an over-correction (one firm not knowing what others are doing) so that a disproportionality one way becomes a disproportionality the other, and an exact equalisation of the profitability of investment in all lines is never achieved.

(vii) *Biased progress*[1]. When technical progress has a capital-using bias the latest superior technique that

[1] This sub-section is difficult and out of proportion to its importance.

offers itself requires a larger expenditure than the last of man-hours of investment-sector labour to equip a man in the commodity sector (the interest bill, representing the cost of waiting is also likely to be greater unless the period of gestation is much shorter). Conversely, with a capital-saving bias the investment per man with each new latest technique is less than with the last.

In these cases it is impossible to realise a golden age, but there may be a quasi-golden age, with capacity output and full-employment output keeping in step, and a constant rate of profit on investment.

A quasi-golden age with a capital-using bias means an ever greater proportion of the labour force going into the investment sector, a rate of growth of output of commodities less than the rate of rise of output per head in the commodity sector and a rate of rise of real wages which is lower not only for this reason but also because, with the growing share of profits, rentier consumption is also increasing.

Conversely, in a capital-saving quasi-golden age the rate of output of commodities, and *a fortiori* the real wage rate, is rising faster than output per head.

From the rentier point of view a capital-using bias is advantageous, but the firms, if they are active and eager investors, prefer a capital-saving bias, for it means that the amount of investment that they can do without depressing real wages is so much the greater.

The change in the cost of investment per man that occurs with biased progress is quite different from that which is introduced by a change in degree of mechanisation when technical progress is neutral. A capital-using bias means that real wages rise less than output per head and a capital-saving bias means that they rise more, while a rise in degree of mechanisation means that real wages rise by more than the golden age rate, and a fall in degree of mechanisation means that they rise by less.

Biased progress introduces very great complexity into the analysis of accumulation. After this hasty glance we shall leave it out of our exercises, and assume that technical progress is always neutral.

(viii) *Income and consumption*

(*a*) *Wages and prices.* One of the conditions of a golden age is that money wages should rise at the same rate as output per head. There is no mechanism in the system to secure that this happens. Wage bargains are made between workers and firms and the balance of bargaining power may be such that money-wage rates rise either less or more than sufficiently to realise golden-age conditions.

When money-wage rates rise faster than productivity, the prices of commodities at full capacity output are raised. If the rentier families keep their consumption of commodities constant, full-capacity prices rise just in proportion to the rise in money-wage rates, so that real wages are unaffected. The firms gain at the expense of the rentiers, for the interest which they owe them on bonds is fixed in terms of money. To maintain their consumption the rentiers have to spend more from given receipts. If the rentier families keep their money expenditure constant, the selling value of commodities rises by the amount of the rise in the wages bill. The firms are neither better nor worse off and the workers gain at the expense of the rentiers. In intermediate cases, firms and workers both gain somewhat, and rentiers lose.

A long continued rise of prices which sets up an expectation of rising prices in the future discourages saving by rentiers (for money which is going to depreciate in purchasing power is not attractive and other forms of wealth are risky and inconvenient). An expectation that money-wage rates will be higher in the future stimulates investment by the firms, each one intending to acquire capital goods, now relatively cheap, which will live into a period when money profits are higher. Rising money-wage rates thus help to make the economy buoyant, but they are highly disagreeable to rentiers and not much good to workers.

When money-wage rates rise less fast than output per head the full-capacity level of prices falls. But unless competition is very active, actual prices may not fall to the full-capacity level. Real wages then rise by less than output per head and effective demand fails to increase sufficiently to maintain capacity output as capacity gradually grows. With surplus capacity emerging in the consumption sector, investment is discouraged, and the economy sinks into stagnation.

It is a curious fact that, though each firm individually hopes to get an advantage by keeping down the wages that it has to pay, for all taken together rising money-wage rates are beneficial, and, indeed, some rise is absolutely necessary to the healthy operation of the system.

(b) *Thriftiness*. As we have seen, a golden age is possible with any constant saving habits of rentiers, but if they grow progressively more thrifty as time goes by one of the essential conditions of a golden age is lacking. When the number of rentier families is constant (or, at least, is increasing less fast than the total of rentier wealth measured in terms of commodities) each is gradually growing richer and it may happen that the ratio of their expenditure to their receipts is gradually falling.

If investment is maintained at the golden age rate, the full-capacity price level for commodities gradually falls and the rate of profit on investment sags. At the same time the ratio of undistributed profits to investment falls and the firms are obliged to borrow more finance from rentiers. This double discouragement means that investment is very unlikely to be maintained.

In so far as investment keeps up, the workers gain from higher real-wage rates but when the rate of investment falls off the workers suffer unemployment immediately and a gradual growth of non-employment as the growth of capacity falls progressively below the golden-age level.

A declining thriftiness of rentiers means rising full-capacity prices, and this may set off an inflationary rise of money-wage rates, but it can be very easily corrected by a reduction in distribution of profits to rentiers (a fall of d to offset a fall of s in our formula, §13.)

24. ADAPTATION TO CHANGE

A once-and-for-all change in the conditions of a golden age may bring into existence another potential golden age and (provided that it does not require a real wage rate below the tolerable level) it is then in principle possible for the system to swing over into the new golden age.

(i) *Deceleration.* Suppose that the rate of growth of population slows down after the economy has for long been progressing smoothly in perfect golden age conditions at the old, higher growth ratio. There are two possible adaptations that the system can make.

One is to keep up the same rate of growth of productive capacity, while speeding up technical progress so as to maintain the old growth ratio. For those who do succeed in getting born this is a better golden age than the former one, for output per head, real wages and rentier wealth are now rising faster than before, and the firms are exerting themselves in a more lively manner.

The alternative adaptation is to pass through a phase of deepening investment (going from Beta to Alpha-plus technique) and then proceeding in a golden age with a higher real-wage rate at any given level of technical development, a slower rate of growth of productive capacity and a lower rate of profit on investment. A worker in this golden age is better off than his opposite number in the old one. The firms once they have got used to the idea of a lower rate of profit on investment are no worse off. The representative rentier may be either better or worse off according to the nature of the technical conditions (the shape of the Beta-Alpha curve); the return per unit of rentier wealth (the rate of interest on new bonds and the yield of shares) has gone down with the rate of profit on investment (assuming an unchanged proportion of profits distributed), but the quantum of rentier wealth increased during the deepening period. The representative rentier is better or worse off according as the rise in the average of rentier wealth is greater or less than the fall in the rate of interest.

Similarly, we can trace out adaptations to a once-and-for-all rise in thriftiness (a rise in the real wage rate and a shift to a higher degree of mechanisation, without any change in the growth ratio), a speeding up of technical progress (a fall in real wages and rise in the growth ratio, so that thereafter they rise faster) and so forth.

Unfortunately, there is no mechanism in the system to make such transitions come about. A fall in the growth ratio or a rise in thriftiness is liable to reduce investment without a corresponding increase in consumption, so that there is unemployment of labour and the economy falls into a state of stagnation, while a rise in the growth ratio, failing to stimulate accumulation, only leads to a growing reserve of non-employed labour.

(ii) *Acceleration.* A rise in the animal spirits of the firms leading to a more rapid rate of investment, if it is accompanied by an adequate speeding up of technical progress, can carry the system into a golden age with a higher growth ratio, but since this requires a temporary fall in the real-wage rate (or, at least, a temporary failure of real wages to rise at the old rate) it may precipitate an inflationary rise of money wages which may frustrate the whole movement. The inflation barrier to speeding up accumulation could be overcome if the distribution of profits were restricted, so as to impose the necessary abstinence upon the rentiers instead of on the workers.

25. PERTURBATIONS

Even if the system does succeed in adapting itself to some long-period change in conditions it is liable to pass through a time of short-period turmoil on the way.

(i) *A boom.* Suppose that something happens in a hitherto golden-age economy to increase the growth ratio and that this is met by an appropriate increase in the rate of investment. Even if there was already full employment it is possible to increase output by working over-time. An increased wages bill in the investment sector means increased demand for commodities The commodity sector is now experiencing a *seller's market*, that is, a situation in which the full-capacity price level is appreciably above the notional full cost of capacity output. Some increase in output occurs through over-time working, etc., but this also swells the wages bill and increases demand. Real wages per hour are now lower, though earnings may have gone up, and a rise in money-wage rates is likely to set in.

All this increases the profitability of investment on the basis of immediate returns, so that, if the situation is expected to last for an appreciable time, the eagerness of the firms to invest is increased. The very fact that they are carrying out investment makes investment seem profitable. The rate of investment is pushed above that appropriate to the initial rise in the growth ratio.

The economy is experiencing an *investment boom*. This is an essentially self-contradictory situation in which the apparent abnormally high profitability of investment is due to nothing else than the abnormally high rate of investment. Such a situation cannot maintain itself, for the stock of plant is growing all the time, and when capacity in the commodity sector begins to increase relatively to demand, the seller's market begins to weaken. The consequent fall in the apparent profitability of investment discourages firms. As soon as they relax the rate of investment, profits fall sharply and the boom breaks.

Thus, if the economy does respond to a rise in the growth ratio, it overdoes it. It overshoots the mark and has to pass through a period of unemployment and low investment till the surplus capacity created in the boom has been digested.

(ii) *A buyer's market.* When something happens to cause a fall in demand for commodities (say, a fall in investment or a rise in thriftiness) the full-capacity level of prices falls. When full-capacity prices are below notional full cost the economy is in the situation of a *buyer's market*. Taken as a whole the firms cannot cover their full costs whatever they do, but each one individually can see that it is bound to lose if it cuts prices, while it hopes that it can retain enough of its customers at the old price level to make it a better policy not to cut. If all (or many) pursue this line of reasoning, prices are not cut to capacity level and output falls. Real wages fail to rise and there is unemployment. The surplus capacity in the commodity sector discourages investment. If price cutting sets in surplus capacity may disappear, but the low rate of return is still damping to the spirits of the firms. When investment falls off, employment and demand fall all the further and the situation becomes still more discouraging.

(iii) *Instability*. Instead of a mechanism to ensure smooth transitions, the system contains mechanisms which exaggerate every change. This inherent instability of the system may set up perturbations of itself even if no long-period change is occurring, so that, even when all the conditions of a golden age are present, harmony is marred by the continuous fluctuations of the trade cycle.

PART THREE

AN EXCHANGE ECONOMY

By commodities we mean goods which are normally bought by households for purposes of consumption. In many respects personal services (repairs of all kinds, waiting in restaurants, etc.) are indistinguishable from goods, but in order to avoid having to repeat the phrase 'goods and services' at every turn we shall confine the exercises to commodities as defined above.

In this group of exercises we are concerned with an economy in which the different types of commodity are given by nature and are distinct from each other both in their qualities from the point of view of consumers and in the means of production required to produce them. In Part Four we shall be concerned with the production of commodities designed by man. The first type corresponds broadly to 'primary products' and the second to manufactures. The distinction in reality is not hard and fast, but, following our usual policy, we make it very sharp in order to clarify the exercises.

If commodities are being exchanged there must be some specialisation in producing them, otherwise each household would be producing for itself. We first consider an economy where the basis of specialisation is the possession of land of particular qualities. Our economy consists of a number of peasant families, each with an inalienable, heritable holding, some well suited to producing one kind of animal, vegetable or mineral product and some another. The peasants meet once a week to exchange their specialities; each sells what he has brought to market and each family consumes what has been purchased within the week, so that there is no carry-over from market to market. There are a large number of families with each speciality and they compete with each other in selling, in the sense that when one finds that he cannot meet with enough buyers he offers his commodity at a lower price in terms of others, to attract custom from his fellow sellers. There are no differences in quality within the supply of each commodity, and no human ties between particular buyers and sellers. An individual buyer therefore will always be attracted to cheaper goods. (It is important to notice that competition in this purely market sense is something quite different from the competition between manufacturing firms that we shall be discussing in Part Four.)

No one commodity is singled out from the rest as money, but three-cornered transactions in the market even out prices, so that, say, a banana seller can get a given quantity of apples for the same number of bananas by trading directly with an apple seller as by first buying, say, coconuts and exchanging them for apples.

I. RELATIVE PRICES

Let us suppose that we examine the market at a particular moment, when a certain pattern of prices is ruling. Each seller has brought to the market a particular quantity of his special product, and the purchasing power that he commands depends upon the prices of other commodities in terms of his speciality.

There are a number of exercises that are easy to do so long as there are not more than three commodities to be considered. We therefore assume that there are three groups of families trading in the market, the Ays who sell apples, the Bees who sell bananas, and the Cees who sell coconuts. The principles derived from the three-commodity case apply to any multi-commodity case which fulfils the same conditions and we need not worry ourselves by thinking out special implications of having such a small number of distinct groups.

First consider the position of a representative man from the Ay group, named Ay-one, who has a certain quantity of apples to sell.

Figure 14(a)

Draw a diagram, marking the origin A, with quantities of bananas measured on the B, or vertical axis, and quantities of coconuts on the C or horizontal axis. The prices for apples confronting the seller-buyer, Ay-one, are such that if he expended his whole stock of apples on bananas alone, he would get AB of bananas (marked on the B axis), and if on coconuts alone he would get AC of coconuts (marked on the C axis). Then the price of bananas in terms of coconuts is AC/AB. The slope of the diagonal BC shows this price. Ay-one is free to buy bananas and coconuts in any combination shown on the line BC. He cannot buy combinations lying to the north-east of BC, for he has not enough purchasing power, and he does not buy any combination to the south-west, for he has been assumed to dispose of all the apples he brought to market.

The diagram represents what we may call the purchasing power at his command, or (if the same situation is repeated from week to week) his real income from trade. He may have other sources of real income—apples which he consumes himself and other home-made products which are not traded.

Figure 14(b)

Draw the same picture for a representative Bee with the origin marked B. We now have apples on the vertical axis, and the quantity of apples that can be bought, at the ruling price, for the whole supply of Bee-one's bananas appears as the distance BA. The coconuts remain on the horizontal axis, and Bee-one's maximum possible purchase of coconuts appears as BC. The price of apples in terms of coconuts is then BC/BA. Similarly a picture can be drawn for Cee-one, with CA and CB as his maximum possible purchases of apples and bananas respectively, and the price of apples in terms of coconuts shown as CB/CA.

Work out some numerical examples, stating what quantity of his commodity Ay-one, Bee-one and Cee-one each bring to market, and giving a consistent set of prices of each in terms of the others. You will find that you can think of any price you like for two pairs of commodities, and that the price of the third pair is then settled.

Given the quantity of his own product that each individual has to sell, his income is determined by its price. This is different from a wage economy, where an individual receives an income in money and all prices are quoted in terms of money. There money income and its purchasing power can vary separately from each other. Here prices and incomes are all of one piece.

We are so much accustomed to think in terms of money prices that to have to think in terms of a pattern of relative prices induces a slight feeling of dizziness. To avoid this, exercises on problems of a market economy are often set out with all prices quoted in one *numéraire*, but this does not really make anything any easier, it only adds another sum to be done in each calculation. Moreover, it is dangerous for two reasons. First, it disguises the real nature of the situation; each seller is interested in the purchasing power of his own commodity, and its price in terms of *numéraire* means no more to him than any other price. Second, it is fatally easy to slip from taking just any commodity chosen at random as a *numéraire* into thinking of it as money in the sense of the medium in terms of which incomes are earned. Anyone who is confident of being able to avoid these dangers may, however, work with a *numéraire* if he likes, say, quoting all prices in terms of apples. The price of apples is then unity.

2. AN INDIVIDUAL IN THE MARKET

To set out the conditions of demand we have to consider how buyers *would* behave *if*—if prices were such and such, and purchasing power such and such, what would Ay-one buy, and Bee-one, and the rest of the Ays and Bees, and the Cees. If prices were such other such, what would each buy? Thus we set out possible combinations of prices and quantities bought. The actual supply conditions will then show which of these possibilities is actually realised.

Figure 14—continued

Take up the diagram for Ay-one and mark in any quantities of bananas and coconuts that you choose to imagine that he is buying. The combination is shown by a point which must lie on the line *BC*, for he is selling no less and no more than his given supply of apples, and all the combinations which exhaust his purchasing power, at the prices shown in the diagram, lie on that line. Let him buy *AM* of bananas and *AN* of coconuts. Let the perpendiculars from the axes at *M* and *N* meet on *BC* at *P*.

We may suppose that we have good reason to believe that he is not acting on a passing whim, nor on any long-range plan affecting his relations with other seller-buyers in the market. We take it that he is reacting in a sensible manner to the immediate choices open to him, and that his behaviour is consistent from one situation to another, in the sense that he would not choose one combination one day and another the next in face of the same relative prices.

The price of bananas in terms of coconuts is, so to speak, the public rate of substitution at which anyone can exchange the two commodities. The fact that Ayone has deliberately chosen a particular combination (shown at P in the diagram) can be taken to indicate that this combination is the one that, in the given conditions, suits him best, for if he had thought that, from his point of view, bananas were worth more in terms of coconuts than is shown in the price he would have increased his purchase of bananas and reduced his purchase of coconuts (so moving P towards B). And conversely. The fact that his choice has fallen where it has may be taken to mean that he is satisfied that he would not be better off if it were somewhere else. This can be expressed by saying that his private rate of substitution between bananas and coconuts, at the combination that he is buying, is equal to the public rate of substitution shown by the price.

Taking him to be a normal kind of consumer, from our general knowledge of how people behave, we can say that for combinations containing more coconuts than the amount he is actually buying and less of bananas, his private rate of substitution would be more favourable to bananas (the more he is buying of one commodity, and the less of the other, the readier he is to swop the first for the second).

Figure 14—continued

If we draw in a curve whose slope shows his private rate of substitution at all points, it will be tangential to the price line *BC* at *P* and it will curl up towards the left, growing steeper as it rises, and down towards the right, growing flatter as it falls. This is known as an *indifference curve*, for it divides all possible quantities of purchases, lying to the north-east of it, which are worth more to the buyer than what he is actually buying from those, lying to the south-west, which are worth less.

It is idle to pretend that we could ever draw up indifference curves even for a single buyer, even if he always had very simple choices to make between only two lines of expenditure. For to find out what combinations he buys at different prices (so as to plot out his private rates of substitution) we should have to observe his behaviour at different times, and there is no guarantee that his tastes and preferences have not changed meanwhile. In fact there is generally a presumption that they have, through the formation of habits. It would not be possible to draw a map if hills and rivers shifted faster than observations could be taken. But the indifference curve is a convenient short-hand way of expressing what we believe that we know about the buyer. For instance, if we happen to know that Ay-one is a man whose family have very rigid tastes, and like to consume bananas and coconuts in a particular proportion (*AM/AN* in the diagram) we can express this by drawing his indifference curve with a sharp corner at the corresponding point (*P* in the diagram). No amount of coconuts above a particular amount (*AN* in the diagram) would compensate for having less bananas than a particular amount (*AM* in the diagram). If we happen to know that they regard bananas and coconuts just as food and that they want more food when they can get it, then the indifference curve is very flat, and the private substitution rates are hardly affected by the combination of commodities being consumed.

Again, so long as the buyer prefers more to less of any commodity—that is, provided it is a good and not a nuisance—a bundle of purchases that contains more of one (compared to another bundle) and no less of the other is worth more to him.

This can be expressed by saying that any point lying to the north-east of the indifference curve through P is on a higher indifference curve (representing a more advantageous level of consumption).

The condition of consistency is expressed by saying that indifference curves never cut, for if one position is both preferred and not preferred by the same man he cannot be obeying the rule of consistent behaviour.

It is a sad mistake to suppose that we can learn anything about human behaviour from indifference curves, but they are sometimes a handy way of expressing what we believe that we know already.

3. INCOME AND DEMAND

We now want to inquire how Ay-one would have behaved if his purchasing power had been different, while the relative prices of the commodities he buys were the same as in the first picture.

Figure 15

In place of a single BC, draw a number of straight lines, B_1C_1, B_2C_2, etc., parallel to each other. As we move up the series, Ay-one is endowed with greater purchasing power—the apples he has to dispose of make it possible to buy more of the other two commodities; his real income is higher in each position as we go up the series in a simple and unambiguous sense. Mark P_1, P_2, etc., to show the combination that he would buy in each position, N_1 and M_1, N_2 and M_2, etc.

If P_1, P_2, etc., lie on a straight line passing through the origin A, the proportion of income spent on each commodity is the same at every level of income. In this case it is said that his *income-elasticity of demand* is equal to unity for each commodity, over the range of income shown.

If P_2 lies to the right of AP_1 produced (nearer to the C axis) and P_3 to the right of AP_2, then the income-elasticity of demand for coconuts is greater than unity (the increase in purchase of coconuts is in a higher proportion than the increase in income) and the income-elasticity of demand for bananas is less than unity; and *vice versa* if P_2 lies to the left of AP_1 produced.

If P_2 lies to the left of N_1P_1 produced, so that AN_2 is less than AN_1, then coconuts are an *inferior good* (like potatoes or margarine) of which less is consumed by a better-to-do family and more by a poor family. If P_2 lies to the right of M_1P_1 produced, bananas are an inferior good.

4. SUBSTITUTION

We have seen the possible relations of demand to different amounts of purchasing power at the same relative prices. We now want to see different prices at the same purchasing power, but this is not so simple. A difference in relative prices means a qualitative difference in purchasing power that cannot be expressed as a simple quantity, so that when prices are different we cannot immediately say what we mean by the 'same' purchasing power. Moreover, the change has a different significance for different individuals

For a single individual, say Ay-one, with a constant quantity of apples to dispose of, we can give a simple definition of what we propose to mean by the 'same' purchasing power, but it is important to remember the qualifications that hedge round this usage.

Figure 14—continued

On the same diagram as before (where Ay-one is buying AM of bananas and AN of coconuts) draw a second price line $B'C'$, so that AC'/AB' is greater than AC/AB (coconuts are cheaper in terms of bananas). If the price line $C'B'$ passes above P, clearly his total purchasing power is higher, for he could buy more than AM bananas without buying less than AN coconuts. (The purchasing power released by the fall in the apple price of coconuts is more than enough to make up for the rise in price of bananas.) Similarly, if $C'B'$ passes below P, his purchasing power is lower. Now assume that we eliminate any change in his total purchasing power by shifting up or down the quantity of apples he has to offer, till with the different income he is just able to buy the same basket, AM bananas and AN coconuts, and cannot buy more of one without buying less of the other. To depict this situation, $C'B'$ passes through P. B' lies below B, and C' beyond C. We now have on one diagram two situations, with two different apple incomes and two different sets of prices, but with the 'same' purchasing power, in the sense that one basket of goods is available in both. This is the basket chosen freely by Ay-one in the first situation. It is the 'same' only if we take that particular situation as the basis of the comparison.

This conception is the one which underlies a 'cost-of-living' index which shows how much money wages would have to be changed to permit workers to buy a particular basket of goods when prices have altered. It is measuring purchasing power in terms of a base-quantity-weighted index.

This is one of several possible ways of measuring purchasing power (the simplest and most convenient) but as it is not the only one we must remember to keep the inverted commas when we say that Ay-one's purchasing power is the 'same' at the two sets of prices and incomes.

The important thing to notice is that while he *can* buy the same basket of goods in both situations, there is no reason why he should.

Figure 14—continued

From the assumption that he acts consistently, with the same tastes in both situations, it follows that he will not buy any combination to the left of P, for when he is free to do so he prefers to be at P. He might have such rigid tastes that only P is any good to him, but generally speaking he will buy more coconuts and less bananas when coconuts are relatively cheaper. The less his private rate of substitution varies with the quantities bought the bigger the difference in the proportions bought. In the limit, if he takes the view that food is food, then he may swing the whole way from buying only bananas, which he finds the cheaper way of getting calories at the price AC/AB to buying only coconuts which he finds cheaper at AC'/AB'.

All this can be neatly illustrated by indifference curves, and it is a useful exercise to draw them in, provided that we remember that we are supplying their properties from our general knowledge of how consumers behave, not learning anything from the shapes that they are assumed to have.

5. WELFARE ECONOMICS

(i) *An individual seller-buyer.* From this root two branches of analysis have grown up. One is called Welfare Economics; this sounds a grand and important subject, but in recent years it has been mainly concerned with a rather narrow problem—the definition of real income.

Figure 14—continued

Redraw the diagram for the individual apple-seller Ay-one with the price of bananas in terms of coconuts AC/AB and Ay-one's purchases shown by the point P. Now we have to consider a comparison with a situation in which the price has changed to AC'/AB'. Draw the new banana-coconut price line so that it passes through P. Let AB' be less than AB. Then AC' is greater than AC. (After completing the exercise it may be useful to work it over again with AB' greater than AB.) Coconuts are lower in price in terms of apples and bananas higher.

In this position Ay-one is not worse off, for, as we have seen, he could buy the same amount as in the first position (AN of coconuts and AM of bananas). If his tastes are very rigid (shown by an indifference curve with an angle at P) he will actually buy the same. But if he likes to take advantage of the relative cheapening of coconuts he is free to do so. Therefore we can say that there is a presumption that he is better off.

If the apple-banana price were such that he could buy more than AB' of bananas he would clearly be better off, for in that case the total purchasing power of his apples would be greater over both the commodities that he buys, so that he could buy all that he bought at P and some more as well.

If the apples that he has to dispose of would buy no more than AC coconuts, clearly he would be worse off, for his purchasing power over coconuts, in that position, is no greater while his purchasing power over bananas is less.

We have now isolated a range of positions, with purchasing power over coconuts between AC and AC' about which we cannot say definitely whether he is worse or better off. In this range he has a lower purchasing power over bananas, but his purchasing power over coconuts is greater. How much this means to him depends on his needs and tastes. If, at the first price (AC/AB) he was perfectly indifferent between bananas and coconuts (shown by his private rate of substitution being equal to the old price ratio for all combinations) the original position of P was quite arbitrary, and with the new prices he will spend his whole income on the cheaper commodity. Thus even if his total purchasing power over coconuts is no greater than AC he is no worse off than he was at P. But this is a limiting case. The presumption is that when (at the new prices) his purchasing power is only a little less than AC he is better off and when it is only a little more than AC' he is worse off.

That is as far as we can take the matter. Moreover, it is as far as the matter can ever be taken on this line of argument, for even if we had unlimited power to experiment, and could offer Ay-one all possible permutations and combinations of prices and purchasing power, we could not deduce from the combinations he bought what is the map of indifference curves that represents his tastes, for the experiments would take time, so that his tastes and circumstances would alter. Moreover, the very fact of the changes going on would react on his tastes. When it comes to the point we have to drop the pretence of high scientific objectivity and rely upon common sense and a knowledge of human nature to assess the situations in which he finds himself.

(ii) *A group of seller-buyers*. So far we have considered the problem from the point of view of a single individual. Now let us suppose that there are differences in tastes among the apple-sellers, though each has the same quantity of apples to dispose of.

Figure 14—continued

In the first diagram, with Ay-one's purchases at P_1, show Ay-two at P_2, buying, say, more bananas and less coconuts than Ay-one, and Ay-three at P_3, buying more coconuts and less bananas. Each is in a position where his private rate of substitution is equal to the public rate shown by the price (AC/AB). We can, if we like, draw in an indifference curve for each, tangential to the price line at the appropriate point.

Now superimpose the position in which the price line, passing through P_1, cuts the B axis in B', below B, and the C axis in C', beyond C. We saw that in this position Ay-one is no worse off and is likely to be somewhat better off. Ay-two (who prefers bananas) is likely to be worse off and Ay-three is clearly better off to a greater extent than Ay-one.

We cannot say that the group as a whole is better or worse off.

Once these principles have been worked out in terms of three groups of seller-buyers we can generalise the argument and apply it to a market in which there are as many commodities as we like, each commodity being subject to the same conditions as the three we have been discussing.

The philosophy behind fixing wages on the basis of a cost-of-living index is as follows. The group of income-receivers is taken to be fairly homogeneous in tastes and needs, so that if, in our example, Ay-one is the representative buyer, who buys commodities in the same proportions as the group as a whole, then the purchases of Ay-two, Ay-three, and all the other members of the group, are clustered round his (so that all the Ps lie close together). Then, when prices are different, a money income that makes it possible to buy Ay-one's combination (shown by P) leaves them in general no worse off.

When in fact individuals in the group have widely different incomes, needs and tastes, this method of measuring purchasing power makes very little sense, but it still may be convenient in some circumstances to accept it as a convention (though, in the above story, Ay-two would feel that the convention was very unfair to him).

6. MARKET DEMAND

(i) *The demand curve.* The second line of analysis developed from the discussion of the individual buyer is that of market demand. Let us consider the position in the market looked at from the point of view of one group, say, the Cees, who sell coconuts. There may be any number of other commodities, a fixed quantity of each one being brought to market every week.

We have seen that a lower price of coconuts is, in general, associated with a larger volume of sales, both because a higher price of other commodities in terms of coconuts means a rise in the purchasing power of the rest of the buyer-sellers taken together, and because when coconuts are relatively cheaper there is a tendency to substitute them for the relatively dearer commodities.

There is a possible exception to this generalisation. If coconuts are a very important part of the purchases of a considerable number of the individuals in the market, so that a lower price of coconuts means an appreciably higher real income for buyers as a whole and if coconuts, from their point of view, are an inferior good (of which less is bought at a higher income) it is possible that the negative income effect may more than offset the positive substitution effect. This is known as the 'Giffen case' because Sir Robert Giffen believed that in his day it applied to wheat.[1] (A high price of bread lowered the real income of the mass of poor consumers so that they were unable to afford meat, and consequently ate all the more bread.) It is quite a useful exercise to work out this case, but we shall not in fact burden ourselves with it. We assume that in the market that we are discussing a lower price is associated with a larger quantity of sales for each commodity taken separately.

Figure 16

We can trace out a market demand curve expressing this relation. On the vertical axis take 'baskets' of all commodities other than coconuts made up in the proportions in which the various commodities are brought to market. On the horizontal axis take coconuts. For each quantity of coconuts mark the price, in baskets of the other goods, at which that quantity of coconuts would be absorbed by the market. The reader is free to draw the curve in whatever way seems to him most natural. For

[1]See Marshall's *Principles*, p. 132.

instance, it may spring from the vertical axis at a price which represents the most that the greatest coconut-lovers are willing to pay for the least conceivable quantity (at a higher price all would feel that coconuts are not worth buying). Near this level large increases in the quantity of coconuts require only slightly lower prices, so that the curve is fairly flat, but as we go along to the right (with larger and larger quantities of coconuts to be disposed of) it sweeps round and down, finally becoming very steep and cutting the horizontal axis at a point where no one would take any more coconuts as a gift.

The curve may have many shapes, according to the nature of the commodity, the habits and tastes of the other buyer-sellers, the dispersion of tastes and incomes amongst them and so forth; the above seems to be the simplest and most general case.

(ii) *Elasticity*. The *price-elasticity* of a curve is a simple mathematical concept which is very handy in analysis. The elasticity is the proportional difference in quantity divided by the proportional difference in price at two positions on the curve.

Figure 17

On a curve which slopes down to the right, compare the position at two points, say at P and, a little lower, at Q. Through P and Q draw a straight line cutting the price axis in p and the quantity in q. Then the elasticity of the curve in respect to that price difference can be represented by Qq/pP.[1] It can easily be seen that, when this ratio is equal to unity, the total receipts from the sale of coconuts is the

[1] See A. P. Lerner, 'A Diagramatic Representation of Elasticity of Demand', *Review of Economic Studies*, Vol. I, No. 1, October 1933. See also *Review of Economic Studies*, Vol. I, No. 3, June 1934.

same in both positions. When the ratio is less than one, the curve is said to be *inelastic* (though this is not quite logical—inelastic means elasticity less than one, not zero). The total proceeds from sales is then less at the lower price. Similarly, when the elasticity is greater than one, proceeds are greater at the lower price. The illustration above, with an appreciable difference between the two prices, is in terms of what is called 'arc elasticity'. When the difference in price is indefinitely small, so that Q coincides with P, the straight line pq is a tangent to the curve at P and shows the 'point elasticity' at P, which is Pq/pP.

The curve suggested above passes through a complete range of point elasticities, from infinity where it leaves the price axis (for here an indefinitely small difference in price changes sales from nothing to something) through a point of unity, down to zero where it cuts the quantity axis.

(iii) *The seller's income*. Our demand curve illustrates a very striking and important fact. Assuming for the moment that Cee families consume other commodities in more or less the average proportions so that the basket of other commodities is a fairly good representation of their real income, we see that an individual seller with a given quantity of coconuts to dispose of is better off the smaller the total number of coconuts sold. A smaller number of coconuts means a higher price, that is a higher purchasing power per coconut, and so a greater income from trade to a seller with a given number of coconuts.

If a greater number of coconuts offered in the market is associated with a larger number per seller, the case is more complicated. When the elasticity of demand over the relevant range is unity it makes no difference to the representative seller, for the larger quantity he has to dispose of just cancels the effect of the lower price. When the demand is elastic the representative seller is better off when he has more to sell. When the demand is inelastic he is worse off. This explains the case of the 'farmer who hanged himself in the expectation of plenty'.

The most favourable situation for an individual to be in is to have plenty to sell himself while belonging to a group with a small total volume of sales.

(iv) *The complex of demand.* We have been measuring the price of coconuts in baskets of other commodities, each basket containing a representative sample of the whole quantity of other commodities sold. A different price of coconuts, however, is likely to be accompanied by different relative prices inside the basket. There are two types of interrelation between prices, one working through income effects and the other through substitution effects.

A high income of the Cees as a group means a high price of those things which they particularly fancy (all supplies being fixed). In our three-commodity world, say, they prefer bananas to apples. Then if a low price of coconuts (associated with a large quantity offered) means a low income for Cees, it is associated with a low price of bananas in terms of apples. The Ays are certainly better off and the Bees are likely to be worse off when the price of coconuts is low. (Thus a low price of rubber is good for motorists and bad for exporters of textiles.)

There would be no effect of this sort if the Cees have a unit income-elasticity of demand for each other commodity, so that whatever happens to Cees' income the relative demands for other commodities is not affected. We can then isolate any effect there may be upon the relative prices of other things that works through substitution. For instance, suppose that the Ays have a low price-elasticity of demand for coconuts and the Bees a price high-elasticity. Then with a lower price of coconuts, Ays spend less apples on coconuts, and have more to spend on bananas, while the Bees have less bananas to spend on apples. The apple-price of bananas is therefore higher when the price of coconuts is low.

When there are more than two commodities for each group of sellers to choose between, further inter-connections can be illustrated. Some commodities may be complementary to each other, like fish and chips, so that a low price for one entails a high demand for the other. Others are close substitutes, like peas and beans, so that a low price for one entails a low demand for the other. Each group benefits by a low price for com-modities which are complementary with its own, and loses by a low price of goods which are close substitutes for its own.

Endless exercises can be devised on these lines. The reader is left to pose and solve them for himself.

When these interrelations between demands are taken into account, we see that there is some difficulty in saying anything about the effect upon the real income per coconut sold of the price of coconuts. The demand curve (so long as all supplies of other things are fixed) can be drawn objectively in terms of baskets of other commodities, but the purchasing power of coconuts over a basket, from the point of view of any individual Cee, depends upon the relation between his particular needs and tastes and the relative prices of goods within the basket. Just now we evaded this difficulty by assuming that the Cees all consume other commodities in more or less the same proportions as those that appear in the basket. In discussing actual cases this assumption is a very useful one provided that we remember that it has been made and correct for any significant departure from it.

On this basis we may continue to draw demand curves, reckoning price in terms of a basket of commodities of a constant composition.

7. MARKET SUPPLY

(i) *Alternative products*. So far we have allowed each family only one tradeable product—the rest of their output has been lumped together as do-it-yourself home production for home consumption. We now introduce a Vee family, which is versatile. With the labour of its members and the land that it occupies, it can produce more than one tradeable commodity. To make exercises simple we will suppose that it can produce no more than two, say apples and bananas.

Figure 18

Take apples on the vertical axis and bananas on the horizontal, with origin O. On the apple axis mark A so that OA is the rate of output per week of apples that the family would produce if all their resources were devoted to apple-production and none to bananas. (We are not bothering about the seasonality of production.) Now consider a position in which a little less than OA of apples is produced and some of the available land and labour used for bananas. (We are making comparisons, not describing events. In each position the outputs of the commodities have long been produced and will continue to be produced without any change in conditions.) Now, a little less apples again, and more bananas, and so on down to the point B on the banana axis, where no apples are produced and all resources are devoted to bananas.

What is the shape of the curve connecting these points? If the land and the labour is all alike and if banana and apple production respond in the same way to differences in the land-labour ratio, AB is a straight line. Apples and bananas are perfectly substitutable for each other from a production point of view in the ratio OA apples to OB bananas, and the ratio is unaffected by the quantities in which they are produced. (We are assuming that there are no economies of large-scale production in either line and no technical advantages from specialising on a single commodity.)

However, even if the land and labour supplied by the family are each perfectly homogeneous, apples and bananas may be supposed to respond differently to different ratios of land and labour devoted to them. At the point A, apples are being produced at the over-all land/labour ratio of the family, and at B, bananas are being produced at that ratio. If land per head were a little higher than this, output per head of each would be greater, but, say, output per head of apples would be proportionately greater by more than bananas per head. Then, when both are being produced, it is sensible to allot a bigger proportion of the land than of the labour to apples. When nearly all resources are devoted to apples, a small change in the proportions of the factors for apples means a big change for bananas, and *vice versa*. Thus as we move along the curve from A, at first a small reduction in output of apples is associated with a relatively large increase of output of bananas; the difference falls off as we move along the curve,

F

and then reverses itself, until, near B, a small increase in output of bananas requires a relatively large reduction in output of apples. The curve therefore bows outwards, being more nearly horizontal close to A and more nearly vertical close to B.

The effect of differences in the composition of output is all the greater if the factors of production are not homogeneous. Thus, when only a small quantity of bananas are being grown, they can all be raised on the best banana land, and when larger quantities are grown land more suited by its nature to apples has to be put under bananas. In the limit, when each kind of land is no use at all for the other crop, only one proportion of apples and bananas can be grown. Then the curve AB is reduced to the rectangle formed by the horizontal from A and the vertical from B.

(This exercise exhibits once more the two forms of *diminishing returns* which we met with in our first Exercises, one due to differences in the proportion of homogeneous factors and the other due to the use of less eligible portions of a non-homogeneous factor as output expands.)

Figure 18—continued

The curve AB expresses the *production possibilities* of the Vee family. At each point it shows the greatest possible amount of apples that can be produced, given the production of bananas, and *vice versa*. At any point on it nothing is being lost for lack of good organisation.

Now draw a tangent to the curve representing the market price ratio of apples and bananas OA'/OB'. Let the tangent touch the curve at P and let Ob ($=aP$) be the corresponding output of bananas and Oa ($=bP$) of apples. Then a, A and A' lie in ascending order on the apple axis, and b, B and B' along the banana axis.

With this market price it suits the family to produce the two commodities in the ratio Oa/Ob, whether they consume them at home or trade them in the market. To produce more apples than Oa for home consumption, would be wasteful; additional apples can be obtained with a smaller sacrifice of bananas by trade (moving along the line $A'B'$) than by switching production (moving along the curve AB). Similarly, it would be wasteful to produce more bananas than Ob.

If they are selling both their products to buy other commodities, the purchasing power of their effort is at its greatest when they produce the two commodities in these proportions.

When the market price ratio is such that one commodity is cheaper in terms of the other in the market than at any combination shown on the production possibility curve, the family will produce only the dearer commodity and buy any they require of the cheaper one in the market.

Figure 18—continued

To illustrate this case, draw a price line through B such that it touches the AB curve at no other point. Then b, P, B and B' all coincide. No apples are produced, for the family finds that it suits them better to specialise entirely on bananas.

(ii) *Elasticity of substitution.* This diagram illustrates a useful device—the *elasticity of substitution*—that is, the proportionate difference in the ratio of the commodities produced divided by the proportionate difference in relative prices with which it is associated. This elasticity is lower the more convex the curve. Thus when AB is a straight line the elasticity is infinite. When there is a right angle at P it is zero.

(iii) *The supply of effort.* So far we have assumed that the resources which a family devotes to producing for the market are independent of prices in the market. Let us now consider cases in which this does not hold.

When the price, say, of bananas in terms of other things, is low they are produced only by Bee families, who have no other tradeable product. If they obtain from the market commodities that are necessary for life, they have to work extremely hard just to keep alive. At a slightly higher price of bananas, they can obtain the same amount of other commodities with less effort, and they may choose to do so. Over a certain range, then, the offer of bananas is less at a higher price and greater at a lower price.

At the other extreme, when the price of bananas is high, all the Vee families who can produce bananas are concentrating on them, and they, as well as Bee families, are enjoying high incomes from trade. Any further consumption of goods purchased in the market may not seem worth bothering about. Thus at a slightly higher price of bananas they do not purchase much more stuff, but take out the benefit in exerting themselves less. Here again a smaller offer is associated with a higher price.

In an intermediate range, between desperation and satiety, it may go the other way, and more effort be called forth by a greater return per unit of effort.

(iv) *Home consumption.* In the first case, when Bees are just struggling to live, they may be supposed to restrain their consumption of their own crop, for every bunch eaten at home then means an important sacrifice of other things.

In the second case, when banana-growers are comfortably off, at a higher price they can afford to eat more and sell less. (This can be expressed by saying that a high income-elasticity of demand for their own product more than offsets the substitution effect of a higher price in terms of other things.)

Home consumption of potentially tradeable products is thus likely to reinforce the effect of differences in effort upon the supply offered on the market.

(v) *A supply curve.* On this basis, we can plot out the relation of the offer of bananas to the price level in terms of other things, assuming that the composition of the basket of other things is not affected by the price of bananas.

Figure 19

Take price on the vertical axis and the quantity of bananas offered in the market on the horizontal axis.

At low prices only Bee families produce bananas. A rise in price is associated with a smaller quantity offered. The supply curve is *backward rising*.

At some point Vee families join in supplying bananas, and the Bees also, now out of the range of desperate poverty, may produce somewhat more at a higher price (though they may also consume more at home). The curve turns through a point of zero elasticity and begins to move up to the right. It is here *forward rising*. Its elasticity over the range is greater (*a*) the greater the response of the offer of bananas by Bee families to a higher price, (*b*) the more the resources of Vee families are attracted to banana production by a higher price, (c) the better suited to banana production the resources so attracted. If over a certain range the elasticity of substitution is infinite (the AB curves for a number of Vee families are straight lines with the same slope) the supply curve is horizontal for a stretch.

At even higher prices, the elasticity of supply grows less. When all Vee families capable of producing bananas are doing so there are no further resources to be called into the business except in so far as extra effort is elicited by a higher return. Beyond a certain point this effect may turn negative and over its highest reaches the curve may again be backward rising.

(vi) *The complex of supply.* For the sake of drawing the supply curve of bananas we assumed that all other things were produced in fixed proportions irrespective of the price of bananas, but there are many cross-connections between the price of any one commodity and the supply of the rest. The following are a few examples.

(a) It may be that a higher proportion of bananas produced by Vee families is not at the expense of all other things in the same proportion, but of one or two that are the nearest substitutes in production—apples in our somewhat fanciful example. A higher price of bananas is then associated with a higher price of apples in terms of all commodities other than these two.

(b) Some commodities are necessarily produced jointly in fairly rigid proportions, for example oil from coconuts and cattle-cake made from the residue. Others are produced from a common source, but are substitutes in production, for instance, a palm that is used to yield toddy bears fewer nuts. Thus a higher demand for coconut-oil which leads to a larger total of palms being grown will increase the supply of cattle-cake, and may either increase or diminish the supply of toddy, according as the effect of substitution more or less than outweighs the effect of a greater total productive capacity.

(c) A higher demand for one commodity may happen to be associated with a lower demand for those which are its closest substitutes in production. In that case the higher demand may be associated with a lower price.

To be able to discuss the supply curve for a single commodity in isolation, it is necessary to find cases in which such linkages as these are unimportant, so that the assumption that the 'other things' in terms of which the price of the commodity in question is reckoned has a fairly definite meaning.

8. SUPPLY AND DEMAND

Assuming that we can measure all other commodities in a standard basket (any differences in the composition of the basket or the relative prices of commodities within it being of no importance), we can confront the demand curve and supply curve for one commodity and find the *equilibrium price* at which supply and demand are equal.

Figure 20

To set out exercises on equilibrium prices, first draw a number of supply curves with one demand curve, then a number of demand curves with one supply curve, and finally, a number of pairs of demand and supply curves.

An intersection between the demand curve with a forward rising stretch of the supply curve gives a position of equilibrium, in the sense that a lower price is impossible, because at a lower price demand would exceed supply, and a higher price is impossible because supply would exceed demand.

It can be seen that a point of intersection of the demand curve with a backward rising stretch of the supply curve shows equilibrium if the slope of the demand curve is less than that of the supply curve (the demand curve cuts the supply curve from left to right as it falls). At this point, a lower price shows an excess and a higher price a deficiency of demand relatively to supply.

The intersection of the demand curve with a backward rising stretch of the supply curve when the slope of the demand curve is steeper than that of the supply curve has no significance, for at this point a lower price means an excess of supply over demand and a higher price an excess of demand over supply. If there is an equilibrium price it must be above or below this intersection (or the curves may cut three times, so that there are two equilibrium points one above and one below).

This method of drawing supply and demand curves for a particular commodity in terms of all the others (or in terms of money representing general purchasing power) is sometimes called the 'partial equilibrium' or 'one-at-a-time' method. Many useful exercises can be done in these terms, but it is important to remember that they exist by courtesy of the assumption that the basket of other things is not affected to any important extent by differences in the price of the commodity that we have picked out to examine, either objectively, in altering the physical composition of the supply of other things, or subjectively, in altering the purchasing power of the incomes of buyers over the particular things that they want to buy.

9. THE GAINS FROM TRADE

A favourite question in economic theory is the gains from trade—that is the advantage to a group of consumer-producers of forming part of a market as opposed to living in isolation. When the market provides a variety of commodities that an isolated group has no means to produce for itself the gains are not easy to evaluate. The question is usually discussed in terms of a situation in which all commodities could in principle be produced in isolation.

Even granted this condition, the question is one of a high degree of abstraction, for a family (or nation) that forms part of a market economy is bound to be affected in its tastes and habits, and is likely to be affected in its techniques of production, by the very fact that it is not isolated. To get the exercise on to its feet we have to imagine that we compare two families exactly alike in every respect except that one has opportunities to trade and the other has not.

To make a simple exercise, consider two Vce families exactly alike, which have the possibility to produce two commodities, apples and bananas, as shown in §7 (i). One lives in isolation, and the other forms part of a market, in which apples and bananas are the only commodities known.

Figure 18—continued

Since our two families have the same production possibility curve, *AB*, we can put them both into the same diagram. The market price line *A'B'*, for the trading family, touches the *AB* curve at *P*, and the trading family is producing two commodities in the corresponding quantities. They are free to consume them in any quantities lying on *A'B'*. Let us suppose they choose the proportion shown by the point *T*, which lies on $A'B'$ above P. They are selling some of their bananas, and consuming more apples than they produce.

Mark H as the point on the AB curve representing the quantities in which the isolated family produces and consumes the two commodities. Draw a straight line from the origin through H to cut $A'B'$ in T'. Along this line the proportion of apples and bananas are the same as at H. T' represents the largest total consumption in this proportion that the trading family can enjoy. Thus HT' provides an indicator (though not a complete measure, as we shall see in a moment) of the benefit enjoyed by the trading family as a consequence of belonging to a market.

Looking at the matter from the point of view of the rest of the economy, bananas are coming from the trading Vee family and apples being sold to it. Drawing the same diagram for the rest of the economy taken as a whole, T lies below P. If the Vee family did not enter into trade the price of bananas would be somewhat higher in terms of apples. The price line would cut OT to the left of T, showing that the rest of the economy would have a somewhat lower real income in terms of the proportion in which it consumes the two commodities when it is able to buy bananas from the Vee family. Thus the possibility of trading with the Vee family is a benefit also to the rest of the economy. (This applies to the rest of the economy taken as a whole. Bee families would be better off and Ay families worse off if this Vee family were out of the market.)

It can be seen that, for any given shape of the AB curve of the Vee family, the distance HT', which indicates the benefit from trade, tends to be greater the bigger the difference between the slope of the price line, $A'B'$, and the slope of the AB curve at H. The latter represents the costs in terms of each other of the two commodities to the isolated family and measures their relative valuations as objects of consumption. The distance HT' represents the additional real income obtainable from trade, measured in terms of commodities in the proportion in which they are consumed in isolation.

If H happened to coincide with P there would be nothing gained from trade. At the other extreme, suppose that H coincides with A, while B' coincides with B. This means that the isolated family consumes nothing but apples and their banana-producing capacity is of no use to them. The trading family finds it profitable to produce nothing but bananas, and can get far more apples for them than the isolated family can get by concentrating all their efforts on producing apples.

This exercise sets out the famous doctrine of *comparitive costs* in its simplest form. The cost of apples in terms of bananas to the isolated family (shown in the diagram by the slope of AB at H) is governed by their comparative costs in terms of the resources available to the family. The price ratio is governed by comparative costs in the market as a whole. The greater the divergence between the two the greater the disadvantage of being isolated.

Figure 18—continued

As we hinted above, the greater real income shown by HT' is not a full measure of the advantage of the trading family. They are free, if they like, to consume apples and bananas in the quantity shown by T', that is, in the same proportions as they are consumed by the isolated family. But with a higher real income and a different price ratio, they may prefer some other combination (T may lie above or below T' on $A'B'$). As we saw in §5(ii) there is an element in this which we cannot quite pin down, but it is evidently an advantage to them, for they need not vary the proportions unless they want to. (The extra advantage of T over T' can be represented by showing that the indifference curve tangential to $A'B'$ at T lies above the indifference curve through T'.)

When apples and bananas are not the only commodities known, the trading family may be exchanging part of its output for third commodities which they cannot produce and the isolated family cannot consume. Here the advantage of trade is something which cannot easily be measured but which, on the basis of common-sense judgment, may be very great. (We assumed the two families to be psychologically alike. If trade awakes desires that were not felt in isolation the benefit may be more dubious.)

10. EQUILIBRIUM AND DISEQUILIBRIUM

(i) *Tranquillity*. In all these exercises we have been taking it for granted that there is a single pattern of prices on each market-day that allows all buyer-sellers to dispose of their goods. This is a large assumption. If all the buyer-sellers turn up in the morning with no idea what to expect and start trading, some will be lucky in finding buyers at what turns out to be above the average price for the day, and these buyers are unlucky. The good and bad luck are passed on to the sellers of commodities from whom these individuals want to buy. Each market-day might be unlike any other, even if all the underlying technical and psychological factors governing supplies and demands never varied.

However, if conditions remain constant for a long time and buyer-sellers learn by experience, we may suppose that they find out the pattern of prices that fits the conditions, and when this is known no buyer will offer more or seller accept less than the equilibrium price appropriate to the transaction in question.

A market where everything has been the same for long enough for equilibrium to have been established, and where it is confidently expected to continue in the same condition for an indefinite future may be said to be dwelling in a state of *tranquillity*.

(ii) *Market equilibrium.* When the market is in equilibrium, a pattern of prices has become established such that the market absorbs the quantity of each commodity that is forthcoming when that pattern of prices rules. Equilibrium means that if the price level in terms of any one commodity were a little higher (that commodity were cheaper) buyers would want more than suppliers are prepared to offer, and if it were a little lower they would not be willing to take as much. Each price affects all demands and supplies and the equilibrium pattern of prices, governed by the technical conditions and the tastes, needs and habits of all the individual buyer-sellers, is such as to secure a fit between demand and supply for each commodity.

When the supply curves for some or all of the commodities are of the serpentine form which we drew in §7(v) there may be several possible positions of equilibrium and which one becomes established is a matter of historical accident.

It is obvious that if the market is in equilibrium in conditions of tranquillity, the pattern of prices, taken in conjunction with technical conditions, must be such that the number of producers of each commodity found in the tranquil unchanging situation can survive and reproduce themselves. This is true only because if it were not so the situation would not be tranquil and unchanging. If, say, the price of coconuts is so low that a representative Cee family cannot live, then equilibrium has not been reached, for the Cee group is shrinking. The existence of equilibrium implies that all elements of disequilibrium have already been liquidated, one way or another, in the course of the past history of the market in question.

The word equilibrium has a soothing and seductive sound, but in this connection it has only a purely formalistic meaning.

(iii) *Oscillations.* A state of perfect tranquillity is very unlike life. Let us now introduce into the story chance fluctuations in the production of various commodities, due, say, to the weather; and shifts in the pattern of demand, due, say, to variations in the needs or tastes of the families of the buyer-sellers who make up the market. When this sort of thing is going on, no one knows exactly what to expect. A market-day may not be long enough to find out the equilibrium pattern of prices for that day, so that sales take place at various prices between morning and evening, and in any case the pattern will be different next time.

Some commodities may fall into definite cycles (like the famous pig cycle) a low price at one market causing a reduced supply offered at the next, therefore a high price, therefore a large offer and a low price at the next market, and so on.

Figure 21

Draw a supply-and-demand diagram with the supply axis running to the left. Using the same vertical axis for price, draw a horizontal axis for time to the right and mark it with an arrow to indicate one-way traffic. Starting from any quantity offered, taken at random, in the left hand diagram show on the right hand side the movement of price through time. Work out what shape and relationship of the supply and demand curves favours a movement of price towards its equilibrium value, and what favours perpetual oscillation.

When a number of commodities are subject to cyclical movements and the cycles are reacting upon each other, pretty well anything may happen and neat generalisations are impossible.

(iv) *Speculation*. In all these exercises we have been working on the assumption that supply reacts to price as though each price that rules is expected to be permanent. In a market subject to oscillations this would be unreasonable. If sellers have a view of what is a normal level of prices for their commodity they will bring more to market, running down stocks, when it is selling above the usual price level, and allow stocks to run up when it is selling below. Moreover, others may take a hand in the speculative game, buying in commodities which seem abnormally cheap in exchange for those that seem abnormally dear, and reversing the operation when the expected price change takes place. This activity has a tendency to iron out the oscillations in prices, by feeding an excess demand out of stocks and absorbing an excess supply into stocks. Clearly, the oscillations cannot be completely eliminated, they can only be mitigated, for if there were no change in prices there would be no gain from the trade and nothing to cover the risk and trouble of holding stocks

All this is upon the assumption that the holders of stocks (whether the producers of the commodity in question or mere dealers) take a correct view of the average around which price fluctuations will occur. If they have no view, or a wrong one, and are guided only by the movements of price, they buy when prices are rising and sell when they are falling, so causing the change that they expect and causing oscillations to be greater than if no speculation took place. Speculation is then influenced by very short-term views, and the stabilising influence of a belief in the average price is undermined.

(v) *Structural change.* So far we have been discussing more or less random ups and downs. Now consider the effect of a large once-for-all change in the pattern of supply and demand.

Figure 20—continued

We can plot out different positions of demand and supply curves as before and then consider what would happen if there was a sudden shift from one position to another. Suppose, for example, that, demand remaining unchanged, there is a sudden rise in output per head of coconuts (owing, say, to the elimination of a pest). When the demand curve is elastic over the stretch between the old and the new equilibrium positions, the income of a representative Cee is raised. When it is inelastic, income is reduced. Prices may have been oscillating before this change occurred, and, even if they were not, a sudden change is likely to set them off. But in any case the level of income round which oscillations occur is now higher.

When demand is elastic, the increase in income will be all the greater if a higher income per unit of effort induces a larger volume of sales per head, for in this case the more the Cees have to sell the greater the total proceeds.

When the demand is inelastic, if the fall in income induces more sales (the supply curve is backward rising) income falls all the more. In such a case there may be nothing to stop the fall in the price of coconuts. (When the demand curve over the relevant stretch is steep and the supply curve backward rising, there is no position of equilibrium shown in the diagram.) Unless something takes place to reduce supply, coconuts cease to yield an income and the Cee families henceforth have to make shift to live from their own produce. If that is not possible, farewell to the Cees.

Similar sad or cheerful stories can be started by changes in demand, the supply curve remaining the same, or by changes in both.

II. MONOPOLY AND MONOPSONY

The market in which each group of sellers is permanently attached to the particular commodity which it has to offer has certain characteristics which work out rather differently in manufacturing industry, where the attachment is not permanent, and we must avoid drawing conclusions from our exercises beyond the sphere to which they apply.

(i) *Restricting sales*. This market, as appears from the exercises that we have already done, is the scene of sharp conflicts of interest. Each individual is better off the more other groups have to offer and the less is offered by other members of his own group. In some cases (where demand for the commodity has an elasticity less than unity) he is better off when his group offers less even if his own offer is a constant proportion of the total. (He gains more of other things in return for less of his own.) It follows that any producers already in a group have a strong interest, in any case, in preventing the group from growing, and in some cases also an interest in an agreement amongst themselves each to limit his offer.

This is the basis of schemes to limit output. Such schemes may be called *monopolistic*, though it is not quite a logical use of language to call the group a monopoly. Any group that makes a monopolistic restriction scheme is doing good to its members at the expense of the rest of the community.

For a group of which every member follows a common policy with complete loyalty, and has no conscience about anyone outside the group, it is possible to work out the offer of their own commodity which yields the maximum return to the group as a whole.

The analysis of this case must be conducted in terms of a comparison between a market in perfectly tranquil conditions where the competitive pattern of prices has long ruled and an equally tranquil market in which the monopolistic price has long been established. The upset to equilibrium of introducing a restriction scheme, or the introduction of a scheme as a result of an upset to equilibrium, involve more complicated stories.

Figure 22

Draw demand curves of various shapes, and find out the corresponding monopolistic offer which maximises the total receipts of the group. It will be seen that at the point corresponding to this offer the elasticity of the demand curve is equal to unity. If members of the group reckon some cost for the time and trouble that they take in producing their saleable commodity (the cost depending upon how much they value leisure or what they could produce for home consumption with the time and natural resources released) they will reduce their offer below the point of unit elasticity of demand. Then, even if the demand curve is elastic at the point corresponding to the offer of the commodity when all members of the group are competing with each other, there is still something to be gained by restriction.

There are two different types of situation in which the motive for forming a monopolistic restriction is very strong. The first is where the difference in total receipts under monopoly and under competition is very large (the arc elasticity of the demand curve between the monopolistic and the competitive point is very low) so that the advantage to each member, if all loyally carry out the scheme, is very great. The second is where the livelihood of the group under competitive conditions is very miserable, so that the difference that it makes to them to have a larger income is very important.

(ii) *Restricting purchases.* Another manner in which one group can gain an advantage for itself at the expense of the rest is by restricting its purchases, that is by artificially lowering its own demand curve for other commodities. This may be called *monopsonistic* action. Where one group forms a significant part of the total demand for the product of some other group, a monopsonistic restriction of demand leads to a fall in the price of that commodity. Where the other group has a backward rising supply curve over the relevant range, a larger quantity can be bought at the lower price. (Third parties also gain, as they find the price of this commodity lowered in terms of their own without having done anything to bring this about.)

In one sense the monopsonistic group is cutting off its nose to spite its face (except in the above case where it actually gets more), for it has to reduce its consumption in order to obtain the benefit of the lower price. But this loss is small where either the commodity in question is regarded as a luxury that can be forgone without real sacrifice or where there is a possibility of producing a home-made substitute which is nearly as good. A general restriction on purchases of everything comes to the same thing as a monopolistic restriction, for it amounts to a refusal to sell the group's own product except at a price above the competitive level.

The desire to gain a monopsonistic advantage is one motive (though only one of several) for the use of tariffs in international trade.

(iii) *Gains and losses*. The use of monopolistic restrictions by one group generally increases the motive for other monopolistic restrictions. One restriction scheme lowers the demand curve (in terms of baskets of the competitive make-up) for each other commodity, and so tends to make it less elastic at the point corresponding to a given quantity sold. (Draw diagrams to verify this point.) It also reduces real income for all other groups. It therefore tends to increase the number of cases where one or other type of motive for forming a monopolistic scheme is strong.

Comparing a market in competitive equilibrium with one in which many are pursuing monopolistic and monopsonistic policies, it is not necessarily the case that the total physical volume of trade is less in the latter case, for it may happen that some groups are in a particularly weak position both in the sense that they find it hard to organise and join in the monopolistic game and in the sense that they have a backward rising supply curve when the price of their product is low. The monopolistic equilibrium then might work out so that they bear the whole brunt—producing and selling more of their commodity (in a desperate effort to get enough of the others to live on) while the other groups sell no less than in the competitive equilibrium.

Generally, however, the monopolistic equilibrium will show a smaller volume of trade in the market than the competitive equilibrium, combined with more home-made consumption or a smaller total of work done.

Many, or perhaps all, individuals are worse off in the monopolistic position, losing more through the restrictions of other groups than they gain through their own. Some, however, may be better off—an increase in their share of the total quantity of purchases being more than sufficient to offset the shrinkage in the total. Moreover, a group finding itself in a market where monopolistic conditions are prevalent and knowing that it would be better off in competitive conditions, cannot, by its own action, remedy the situation, for merely to forswear restriction itself would only weaken its position. What it wants is for all groups to forswear restriction. But those who believe that they gain from their own restrictions more than they lose from others', and those who are not too badly off and fear a change, will never agree.

It appears then that (in a market of this kind) where (1) individuals feel a sense of loyalty to the group to which they belong, (2) purely economic motives dictate policy, (3) the formation of restriction schemes is possible, competitive conditions will never prevail.

12. A PLEASING FANCY

Is it possible to say anything about the advantage to the economy as a whole of maintaining competitive conditions?

So long as there are conflicts of interest it is not easy to see what the 'general good' can be taken to mean, but we can explore the question in terms of a harmonious economy in which each individual accepts the position in which the rules of society place him and does not protest or try to change the rules, and in which all individuals are sufficiently alike to have similar views as to what is desirable.

Let us suppose the whole economy consists of one family which has certain resources to dispose of and a variety of commodities that can be produced. It is too large and complex to manage its affairs without some accounting procedure, and it works on a system which simulates the operations of a market. Each individual is allocated a notional income and asked to say how he would divide his expenditure between different commodities at different prices. A production plan is then drawn up so that the supply of each commodity is equal to the demand for it.

The case where there are only two possible commodities can be illustrated by the diagram that we used for the Vee family.

Figure 18—continued

AB is the production-possibility curve with a given total of work performed by the members of the family (the principles upon which the amount of work should be fixed is another story). It is impossible to produce any combination of apples and bananas outside AB, and to produce at any point inside the curve means unused resources. Production, therefore, will be somewhere on the curve, the exact position being governed by the demands of individual members of the family. The notional incomes distributed to the members of the family may be reckoned in terms of apples. The total income is set at OA.

Now draw any price line, taken at random, as a tangent to AB at P^1. Draw perpendiculars to the axes, P^1a^1 and P^1b^1. Then Oa^1 and Ob^1 are the rates of production of the commodities corresponding to P^1. If total demand, at this price of bananas in terms of apples, comes to either more apples than Oa^1 or more bananas than Ob^1 the demand cannot be satisfied, and the price must be lowered or raised, as the case may be. By this method a price is found such that when the tangent is at P, Pa and Pb represent the quantities demanded at that price. These quantities are then put into production and the demands are met.

Since all members of the family are taken to be fairly alike in their tastes and needs, and since we go on the assumption that each knows what he wants and does not regret the choices that he has made when his demands come to be met, we can say that in this position the family as a whole is doing better for itself, with its given resources, than it could in any other. The fact that the chosen output (P in the diagram) lies on the production possibility curve shows that it is not possible to get any more of either commodity without producing less of the other, and the fact that the representative individual has freely chosen to consume the commodities in these proportions is taken to show that he prefers these proportions to any other combination.

Figure 18—continued

Since individuals are alike, we can draw a combined indifference curve for them, and show it tangential to the price line at P. This expresses the fact that, for any one individual, the sacrifice of bananas required to get a few more apples would be greater than the benefit from having more apples, and *vice versa*, so that he is best off where he is.

In this situation we can say that the family as a whole is getting the greatest benefit possible from its given resources. The distribution of income amongst them has been settled on principles which are unquestioningly accepted. They are consuming commodities in the proportions that they prefer, and the quantity consumed, in those proportions, is as large as it is physically possible to make it in the given conditions. If we compare their position with one in which the same productive resources have been manipulated by monopolistic groups, it is clear that their imitation competitive market is giving them a more satisfactory result.

When individuals differ very much in their tastes, we cannot say that the position arrived at in this way is the best from a collective point of view in any simple and clear sense, for there is then no such thing as a consistent collective point of view. For instance, a man who is particularly keen on bananas is better off if others prefer apples, so that bananas are relatively cheap. There is no way of setting the drawback, from his point of view, that others consume bananas against the benefit to them of being free to do so.

Harmony, however, prevails for all accept the system that they have adopted as fair and reasonable, and abide by the arbitrament of the notional market which fixes the purchasing power of their allotted incomes, even though it may not be the same, from a subjective point of view, for each of them individually.

13. PRICES AND POLITICS

The foregoing fantasy, in which the distribution of wealth and income between individuals is arranged on a generally acceptable plan, cannot throw much light on the problems of a market economy in which families, endowed with arbitrary amounts of productive capacity suited to particular commodities, find that the distribution of income between them largely depends upon the scarcity relatively to demand of the commodities that each is able to supply. In such a case there is no simple criterion for the 'general good' and no obvious sense in which it can be said that the arbitrament of a free competitive market ought to be universally acceptable.

(i) *Social justice*. If all form part of a single political community (whether a nation or a group of nations subject to a common 'world opinion') imbued with modern democratic notions of social justice, the view is likely to prevail that, in principle, those in a favourable position should not be allowed to indulge in restrictions to make themselves still more wealthy and that those in a weak position should somehow be helped. An upholder of the free-market ideal will maintain that they should not be allowed to help themselves by a restriction scheme, for in that case the burden of helping them is thrown on to their customers in an arbitrary manner. It should be arranged so that the whole community contributes in an equitable way. But the means to arrange this may not be easy to find and the rough justice of a restriction scheme to raise intolerably low incomes may be the best that comes to hand.

This may be generally agreed in principle, but in practice it is usually the strong sellers who are best able to pull political strings in their own favour.

(ii) *Buffer stocks*. A market of the kind that we are discussing is subject to constant oscillations of prices, which are a great nuisance to all concerned. As we saw, they may be damped by speculation provided that speculators make tolerably correct estimates of the equilibrium pattern of prices and are prepared to take moderately long-term views. But even the best behaved speculators must allow considerable oscillations to continue. There is therefore a case for some public authority to operate in the interests of the market as a whole to abate the nuisance of fluctuating prices.

(iii) *Emergencies*. A free market in a world subject to structural changes produces from time to time disastrous situations for particular groups, as we saw in the case where the bottom fell out of the market for coconuts (§10(v)). In a case of this kind it would obviously be vain to preach the benefits of a free market to the sufferers. If they have any kind of political power to help themselves, they will use it; and 'world opinion' cannot condemn them unless it has some better remedy to offer.

PART FOUR

CAPITALIST INDUSTRY

I. INTRODUCTION

WHEN we turn from a world of natural commodities and factors of production to modern manufacturing industry the neat concepts with which we have been operating dissolve into a haze. Man-made commodities (especially in the present age of synthetic materials) cannot be sharply demarcated according to their technical nature (are rubber and leather shoes one commodity?) nor, when the standard of life is above bare necessities, according to the wants they meet (are tennis shoes to be classed as 'footwear' or 'sports equipment'?). Moreover, wants themselves become blurred under the impact of advertisement and sales pressure.

Producers and sellers normally handle a certain range of commodities, not only one. The attachment of a group of producers to any commodity is only temporary —workers can shift and plant be adapted to produce totally different lines of goods as one becomes more profitable than another.

Competition between sellers is not confined to offering an identical commodity at a lower price, but enters into the design of the commodity itself, as well as into all the multifarious forms of enticements to buy with which it is surrounded. The conditions of demand and supply are never, and are never expected to be, unchanging from week to week and year to year, but are in a continuous state of flux.

167

Above all, the relation between prices and incomes is radically different. In the exchange economy each group of producers is specialised to a particular commodity and the incomes of individuals are governed by the price of their commodities. In manufacturing industry specialisation is only a matter of time, for a labour force accustomed to mechanised production of any kind can readily learn any other, and financial resources can be embodied in any kind of equipment. Because of this potential fluidity of factors of production, each industry has to offer prospects of earnings at about the same level as all the others, in order to obtain the factors it requires.

The general rate of profit on investment, as we have seen in Part Two, depends upon the general development of the economy; as between one industry and another, the level of prices has to be such as to promise profit at more or less the general rate if it is to retain its productive capacity. The incomes of capitalists depend, in the main, simply on the amount of capital that each commands, not upon the particular type of productive capacity in which it has been invested.

Different wage levels may be established for different classes of workers. There is a general tendency for wage levels to be higher for jobs requiring special training and, in a developing economy which has been enjoying a reasonably high level of employment for some time, for those which are generally regarded as unpleasant, for otherwise they could not attract workers. (In conditions of chronic unemployment it is the other way round and the least eligible jobs are usually the worst paid.) For production to be profitable, prices have to cover costs, and differences in wages are reflected in differences in prices. The pattern of demand in various markets influences the pattern of production and (apart from unforeseen perturbations) has little effect upon prices; just the opposite of the situation in which the pattern of supply is given more or less rigidly by nature, and prices are governed by the pattern of demand.

Thus, broadly speaking, in an industrial economy, incomes govern prices, rather than prices governing incomes. The exception, which proves the rule, is the case of primary products, where a whole community depend for their living upon means of production provided by nature in a specialised form—mineral deposits or soil and climate appropriate to a particular crop. Here price is strongly influenced by the relation of demand to supply, and price is the main influence upon the incomes of the producers. For this type of production the analysis of the exchange economy is relevant, and the morals which we drew from it are painfully true of primary producers in the world to-day.

Instead of attempting, as many economists have done (not excluding myself), to force the amorphous products of industry into the neat pigeon-holes appropriate to natural commodities, it is better to start afresh with a different set of categories.

2. INDUSTRIES AND MARKETS, FIRMS AND PLANTS

Manufactured products can be classified according to the market they supply, so that we treat as near-enough the same commodity things which are close substitutes for each other from the buyer's point of view. Products from different manufacturers are never quite interchangeable, for each source of supply has its own style, its own reputation for reliability and so forth, and its own geographical location. At the same time, everything, in a certain sense, competes with everything else as a possible object of expenditure. It is all a matter of degree. In a rough and ready common-sense way we can map out the whole flow of production into distinct markets, looking at the matter from the point of view of demand, in such a way that commodities offered within a market are closer substitutes for each other than is any commodity classed as being outside the supply to that market.

In a similar rough and ready way manufactures can be grouped into industries having in common a method of production, whether dictated by the material used, the kind of technique or the kind of object produced. The manufacturing firms making up a single industry are generally serving a number of markets. For instance, there is no substitutibility on the demand side between, say, tennis balls and tyres, between men's and women's shoes, or between tractors and motor scooters. The boundaries of an industry are drawn by the criterion that productive capacity can be switched from one line of production to another within it more easily than across the boundary. This depends partly upon the range of versatility of the equipment in existence and partly upon the corpus of technical know-how available to the firms concerned, but it also depends upon their commercial connections, so that commodities may be produced together for no other reason than that it is convenient or customary to sell them together.

The productive capacity of an industry at any moment consists of certain establishments, each a distinct entity such as a factory, equipped for a certain range of production and capable of offering employment to an appropriate labour force. The establishments, or *plants* for short, are controlled by firms which we take to have the general characteristics mentioned in Part Two §9.

A firm may control one or many plants and one firm often has a footing in several industries. For the consideration of questions concerning production a plant is a more convenient unit than a firm, while the firm is the appropriate unit for considering questions of policy and the earning and disposal of profits.

Each of the plants may be serving a number of distinct markets. In some of the markets that it serves the firm which controls it may have no close rivals; in others it is in more or less active competition with fellow manufacturers in the same industry; in some it may have to contend not only with members of the same industry but also with substitutes produced by members of quite different industries.

The number of firms in a particular industry at any moment is largely a matter of historical accident. In those which are easy to enter on a small scale, numbers may have been stable for some time or even growing, but it is never possible to predict how long this state of affairs will last, for at any moment technical change or the emergence of an ambitious empire-builder may start a process of concentration. Sometimes a few firms have been growing faster than the industry, absorbing others, or competing them out of existence. A single giant may already be in possession of the field or the process of concentration may have been checked when two or three survivors are afraid to challenge each other to the last fight. Often the large firms are surrounded by a fringe of small ones whose existence they tolerate, and from time to time a new challenger appears who succeeds in establishing himself as a serious rival.

The degree of concentration in an industry, in the sense of the size of the firms that compose it relatively to its total output, is not the same thing as the extent of monopoly in the markets which it serves. An industry which is very little concentrated, being composed of a large number of relatively small firms, may contain several quite strong monopolies of particular products, while another may be composed of only two or three firms which are in quite close competition in all of the markets that they supply, with each other and with the products of other industries.

None of this lends itself easily to simple exercises; it requires rather to be treated in terms of a natural history study of the behaviour of various types of firm in various environments. Nevertheless we must try to peer into the general development of an economy such as we discussed in Part Two to see something of the detail of its operation, for the movements of the whole are the product of interactions between the movements of the parts.

3. INDUSTRIES IN A GOLDEN AGE

In the golden age depicted in Part Two all commodities were consumed in constant proportions and all industries expanded together; this was a simplification to keep out of the way questions which we now want to discuss. We can imagine an over-all golden age in which different industries, roughly but sufficiently demarcated in the manner discussed above (§2), are growing at different rates. An industry grows at more than the general rate when the income elasticity for its range of products (taken as a whole) is greater than unity, so that a more than proportionate share of the growing total of demand is coming its way. And it may grow at more than the over-all rate if it has a rapid rate of technical progress so that costs of old products are falling and being pushed into increased consumption by lower prices and new products that attract demand are being introduced.

In either case profits realised in the industry are likely to be higher than the general rate; in the first case demand may be expanding a step ahead of supply so that a seller's market is being enjoyed; in the second case costs are falling a step ahead of prices, so that high profit margins are being enjoyed. The high profits provide fuel for the expansion, partly by firms financing their own investment and partly by making borrowing easy. At the same time the high prospect of profit is attracting new, active, go-ahead firms, and enlivening old ones.

Differences between industries in the level of profits depend very much upon the ease with which new competitors can come in. If all industries were equally easy to enter on a small scale, very small differences in prospective profits would be sufficient to steer investment into those which are expanding and consequently to keep prospective profits from rising much above the general level. On the other hand where there are impediments to investment (limited natural resources, monopolistic restriction or a large minimum scale of investment) prospective profits may be higher than the average even in industries where no expansion is going on.

Differences in levels of profitability are perfectly compatible with tranquil conditions, but a change— say, an increase in the severity of the obstacles that monopolistic firms put in the way of would-be competitors—may react upon the over-all rate of investment and so cause perturbations.

After a period of more than average growth, an industry may sink to the general level or below it. If this is foreseen in good time investment will be tapered off smoothly (meanwhile the over-all golden age may be maintained by other industries going into a phase of high expansion) but if it takes place through an over-shoot (such as we referred to in Part Two §25), leaving an excess of capacity relatively to demand, it interrupts the harmony of a golden age and may even precipitate a general slump.

Within an industry which is expanding, we can imagine each firm remaining at a constant size and the number growing with the growth of output; or each firm may grow to a certain size and then stabilise, so that over any period growth is partly through the expansion of middle-aged firms and partly from new births; the number of firms may be constant and each growing in about the same proportion as the industry; or the number of firms may be falling, the most ambitious and successful killing off or buying up more feeble rivals or amalgamating with their peers. In any case productive capacity is increasing and this happens partly by new plants being set up (whether by old or new firms), partly by enlargements of old ones (which may or may not have been changing hands between firms) and partly by the technical improvements which are being introduced.

A common case, in a technically progressive industry, is one in which the number of plants is growing while the number of firms is falling.

Some industries may be stationary within a golden age, and a situation in which productive capacity has to be reduced and can be reduced without loss, is not in principle impossible. In practice a reduction in capacity usually indicates a mistaken investment in the past, which is not compatible with golden age conditions.

When stationary industries are making profits they are, directly or indirectly, lending their savings to finance investment in other industries which are expanding fast enough to absorb more investible resources than their own savings provide. This may come about by firms in a stationary industry investing directly in an expanding one, setting up plants to produce its type of product and invading its markets; or the stationary firms may be lending to the rest of the economy by amassing financial reserves; in either case, any savings by individuals who draw income from the industry are being absorbed by investment in others.

Labour is moving into industries where output is growing faster than output per head.

In this way the relative positions of different industries and the relative positions of firms within an industry, may be changing without disrupting over-all tranquillity.

In untranquil conditions, the various vicissitudes of a developing economy which we referred to at the end of Part Two strike different industries differently; some may be flourishing while most slump and *vice versa*; but both conditions are contagious, for a rise or fall of expenditure at any point affects incomes all round; the vicissitudes of any one important industry are liable to infect the whole economy.

4. PROCEEDS AND COSTS

In tranquil conditions, when expectations are being realised, proceeds from the sale of the output of a plant, over, say, a year, are sufficient to cover all its actual outgoings, an allowance for amortisation and a net profit from which the firm pays interest and dividends, finances its own investment or amasses reserves. To see how this comes about we must look at the situation when expectations are being formed.

A firm which is considering making an investment has to consider what is the best use to which it can put the finance involved. The range of commodities which it can contemplate producing is more or less strictly limited by the technical knowledge and experience of its staff, its commercial connections and so on. Amongst these possibilities it is especially attracted to any where it believes itself to have some advantage over rivals or a new idea that has not yet been exploited by others; where all that is open to it is the well-known "bread and butter" of the industry that it belongs to, it thinks first of those lines in which demand seems to be unsatisfied at the moment or promising to expand in the near future.

Having picked a hypothetical type of output it considers what proceeds may be expected. Here the question of prices comes in. For bread-and-butter lines there is a price already ruling in the market; prices to the final buyer and the range of discounts necessary to offer to dealers are established. The firm has little room for manoeuvre and takes the prices that it would be possible to charge as given by market conditions. To break into a market where it has not sold before it may have to offer larger discounts or undertake special selling costs. Cutting price to the final consumer is a dangerous game which invites retaliation much more openly than the hidden pressures of salesmanship; it is, moreover, frowned upon by its fellows in the industry and, though it is competing with them, it may not feel inclined to brave their ill will.

Where it has some specialities that differentiate its proposed output from that of others, it has to consider the best prices to set on them. This is the subject that gets most of the limelight in the text books, but business men usually dismiss it by saying: 'Of course, the price has to be right'; that is, a price must look reasonable in relation to other commodities in the same field—not so high as to put it at a competitive disadvantage and not so low as to waste potential revenue. No doubt "business instinct" has more to do with the matter than nice calculations, though in some cases market research is brought into play to help provide data for the decision.

Where the firm has something quite new in mind— say, a substitute for an old commodity which is dramatically cheaper to produce and is protected from imitators by a patent or by technical secrecy—the firm has a wider range of possible policies. It may choose a price for the new commodity on the basis of the old one, so that it carries a very high profit margin for the time being (possibly being prepared to cut drastically later) or it may take advantage of low costs to go out for a low price and rapid sales.

Having set out the hypothesis about prices, the firm has to consider what volume of sales it may expect from the new plant, what selling costs it will have to incur to get them, how long they are likely to last and what possibilities there will be of turning the plant over to other uses when the first one ceases to be profitable.

Having thus formed some hypothesis about the prospects of proceeds, it considers the future flow of costs and the time over which the investment should be amortised.

The scale of the investment may be determined by technical considerations; if the firm is a powerful one with ample finance available it will choose a plant of what it believes to be the most efficient size for the job in question. If it is limited by finance it may have to be content with something less, and so incur higher costs and enjoy smaller profit margins than larger rivals, hoping to be able to grow out of realised profits and achieve the technically optimum scale later on.

It must consider the prospective course of costs over the lifetime of the investment; whether technical improvements will be possible within its framework; what is likely to be the course of wage rates, prices of materials, power, etc.

Now, comparing expected proceeds and expected costs, it has to decide whether the investment will yield a profit, first, sufficient to justify the investment, and second, better than alternatives that are open to it.

When the sum turns out unfavourable the firm abandons this project and looks round for some other scheme in which, with its particular advantages and weaknesses, it can expect to find a line where costs will fall short of proceeds by a sufficient margin.

All this may be done by careful calculation or just on hunch. In either case the essential point is to find an investment where the costs likely to be incurred seem to be less than the proceeds likely to be enjoyed by a sufficient margin to make the project seem attractive.

Once the plant exists, it has to take what comes, and the return that it actually yields may be better or worse than what was expected. It will have to adapt itself as best it may to unforeseen changes (this is discussed below, §8–10). Meanwhile its existence, and the policy of the firm controlling it, is playing a part in the markets that it serves in determining the profitability of investment by others.

The search which firms keep up, as investment goes on, for the most profitable line of advance, keeps costs and prices more or less in line with each other, for prices high relatively to costs is a signal for investment to come in and enlarge capacity. But on the whole it would be more true to say that market prices for particular commodities determine their costs of production than that costs determine prices, for the costs that it is worth while to undertake, for any individual producer, depend upon the prices that he expects to be able to charge.

5. COSTS AND PRICES

It is easy to say that, by and large, proceeds exceed costs of production in normal conditions, but it is by no means an easy matter to pin down the cost of production of a particular batch of output to compare it with the price at which it sells.

(i) *Overhead costs*. The first difficulty is that the cost of the output being produced at any particular moment is not independent of output at other times. It is usually possible to distinguish for the product of a particular plant, say, for a week, the *prime costs* which are involved in that particular output (wages of workers that could have been dismissed if that output had not been produced, power, materials, etc.). But cost also includes a due share of the *overheads*, general expenses of the business, not attached to any particular week's output, including the wages or salaries of employees who cannot be dismissed and taken on again with changes in the rate of output, and including cost of repairs and maintenance, and a due share of amortisation charges on buildings and equipment; there must also be a due contribution to net profit (out of which the firm concerned may be required to pay interest on finance borrowed from outside).

A firm is usually committed to the general costs of running a plant for at least a year (often much longer) and amortisation and profits are to be spread over the whole life of the investment concerned. The load appropriate to any one week's output depends upon how many other weeks are to share it, and the calculation of the cost of a particular week's output involves estimates of technical and market conditions for months and years ahead.

(ii) *Swings and roundabouts*. Any particular week's output from a plant is generally made up of a number of products (often to be sold in quite distinct markets). They are attached to each other sometimes for technical reasons, because they are conveniently produced together (for instance because one uses a by-product of another), sometimes for commercial reasons, because it is easier to sell small quantities of a number of things than large quantities of one, and sometimes for a mixture of the two.

In such cases the share of each product in general overheads or in the cost of processes that they have in common does not have an unambiguous meaning. Firms may find it convenient for certain purposes to 'allocate' costs according to some convention, such as the share of a particular product in total receipts, or in labour costs, or in the floor space occupied, but the very fact that the same situation can be presented in various ways, according to the convention adopted, shows that the notion of individual costs has no particular meaning. It is not that 'What's lost upon the roundabouts we pulls up on the swings' (for, if so, why not scrap the roundabouts?) but that the profit made from both together cannot be attributed to either alone. (If there were no roundabouts, fewer people would come to the fair, and less would be made on the swings.)

(iii) *Stages of production*. A single plant is generally concerned with a particular stage of production, and buys in materials and components from outside. It is also usually dependent on outside sources for power and transport. The prices of all these things enter into its prime costs. They also enter into the investment in working capital on which the firm concerned expects to earn profits. Since the prices contain an element of profit, there is a compounding of profit on profit over the process of production. If all firms were equally efficient and a uniform rate of profit on investments were being earned throughout the economy, it would not make any difference how the various stages and various elements were distributed amongst firms; in equilibrium (when expected profits are being earned) a firm which covers several stages of production is receiving, in the final prices at which it sells, profits on the capital invested, corresponding to compound interest (at the ruling rate of profit) over the period of time occupied by all these stages, just as it would if it bought from another firm at the end of a stage and included the outlay in its investment in working capital for the next stage.

But when firms vary in efficiency or the rate of profit is not uniform, the pattern of inter-firm transactions has an important influence on costs. For instance, the effect of a high price, due to monopolistic influences, for an element in an early stage of production, is compounded up through later stages and has a larger effect on final selling prices than if it had occurred near the end of the process.

(iv) *Selling costs.* Generally speaking, the problems which most concern the firms are problems of marketing rather than of production, and competition in selling is nowadays the dominant form of competition. Selling costs can sometimes be separated from production costs but very often they are inextricably interwoven with each other, and from the firm's point of view the distinction between them is not of any great significance.

(v) *The spread of costs*. The plants producing overlapping ranges of varieties of commodities, selling in competition with each other in the markets which they serve, may have widely different costs. An outstandingly low-cost plant may have some permanent advantage, such as a convenient site, or it may be controlled by a particularly efficient firm, or it may have been set up, or reconditioned, recently so that it embodies the latest, most superior technique, and is for the moment at the head of the line in the leap-frog game of technical progress. High cost, conversely, may be due to special drawbacks such as inefficiency or obsolescent equipment, or it may be due to the plant being too small to enjoy all the technical economies of scale, because the firm controlling it was not able to command enough finance to set it up at the most efficient size. (A small business producing high quality or bespoke work is not to be classed with high-cost producers; it is producing a substantially different range of commodities that happen to be called by the same name as mass-produced articles, but are not in close competition with them.)

(vi) *Prices*. Manufactures are not sold, like the apples and coconuts of our exercises, by carrying them to market and taking what they fetch. The producer has to declare his prices (or arrive at them by bargaining with traders) and sell what will go. A businessman will usually say (and some economists have taken it literally) that prices are fixed by costs of production but this cannot be true, in any simple sense, for three sets of reasons. First, as we have seen, the cost of any particular item, in any particular week, cannot be calculated separately from the other items that are produced with it that week or from total production over the whole life of the plant. Secondly, even if the relevant total costs have been estimated, the question of the total allowance for profit and its allocation between various items is left in the air. (The business-man tells us that he includes, along with costs, a reason-able allowance for profit, but that does not take us much further.) Thirdly, prices cannot be fixed by costs alone, without regard to market conditions. The business man does not really expect us to believe that he first incurs some costs and then fixes prices to cover them without any inquiry into the state of demand.

As we have seen (apart from exceptional cases where a firm has a wide choice of possible policies) the main influence on the prices set by any one firm is the prices that have already been set by others. For each firm (even when competition is very imperfect) prices are more or less narrowly determined by market conditions, and its business is not to fix prices to cover costs but to find things to produce at costs which make the given prices profitable.

The relation between costs and prices is much more complex, subtle and varied than either the businessman or the economic text book is ready to admit.

6. NORMAL COST

To formulate exercises we must simplify the argument a great deal.

We first consider the situation of a firm, in tranquil conditions, which is realising the proceeds and costs that were expected when it made an investment in a particular plant.

To be able to set out an exercise in a diagram we have to reduce the complexities of actual situations to terms that can be dealt with in two dimensions.

(*a*) We are concerned with a self-contained plant whose operations are independent of any other controlled by the same firm.

(*b*) Its output is homogeneous both in a physical sense and in the price realised per physical unit.

(*c*) Decisions have already been taken as to the price to be charged and the amount of selling costs to be incurred.

(*d*) The firm has a clear view as to the length of time over which investment must be amortised.

(*e*) The present situation is expected to last for some time.

The diagram is usually drawn in terms of average and marginal cost per unit of output, so that total cost appears as the area of a rectangle. For our present purposes it is more convenient to show total cost as a length and average and marginal costs as slopes (as in Figure 1*b* in Part One §1). We can then set up an adaptation of the 'break-even' diagram which is much used in business but has only recently begun to penetrate into economic analysis.[1] Anyone familiar with the traditional diagram can readily translate from one to the other.

In the case to be illustrated, we take it that the firm has a definite view as to the share, say per week, in overhead cost and in the contribution to gross profit (amortisation plus net profit) that the plant is expected to be contributing at this time in its life. (The expected contribution generally varies with the age of the plant.) This sum is independent of the rate of output. Prime

[1] I am indebted for this device to D. R. C. Halford, *Differential Costs and Management Decisions*.

costs partly vary with output but there are some lumpy elements which have to be incurred if any output is to be produced and which do not increase proportionately to output. Moreover, when the product is made up of an assemblage of parts there is a particular rate of output at which they have been organised to fit, so that other rates of output are awkward and involve higher average prime cost. On the other hand, for rates of output greater than that for which the plant was designed, some elements in cost rise with output (over-time pay, lack of pauses for clearing up, wearing out machinery by faster running, etc.); thus after a certain point average prime cost rises with output, and short-period marginal cost rises above average prime cost.

As the absolute physical limit of capacity is approached, marginal cost rises very sharply, but what the firm regards as the normal capacity of the plant is generally well short of the maximum physically possible rate of output; plants are generally constructed so as to be capable of a higher rate of output than is expected to rule most of the time, in order to leave room for sudden rush orders, standby capacity in case of breakdowns, and so forth. Where it is not strictly dictated by technical conditions, 'normal capacity', like average total cost, is partly a subjective concept, depending on the expectations and policies of the firm concerned. For convenience we will assume that, in the case that we are illustrating, there is a fairly definite capacity output given by purely technical conditions, at which average prime cost per unit of output is at a minimum.

The amount of selling cost which it is necessary, or in the firm's view appropriate, to incur, may also be divided into overhead and prime elements—the overhead part being outlays such as a general advertising campaign, which do not vary with sales, and the prime element being those, such as salesmen's commissions, which do. We include in normal costs the amount of selling costs that the firm considers requisite to enable it to dispose of the capacity output of the plant when the price which it has chosen is ruling.

Figure 23

Take flows of money per week on the vertical axis and output per week in units of the homogenous commodity on the horizontal axis. From the origin O, the distance OG on the money axis represents the week's share in overhead cost and gross profit at what the firm reckons as the correct rate. This is the same for all rates of output and is shown by a perpendicular to the money axis at G parallel to the output axis. Take a point above G to represent the fixed element in prime cost. From this point draw a curve rising to the right to show total costs corresponding to each level of output. The veritcal distance of a point on this curve above the G line shows the prime cost of a week's output at the corresponding level. If prime cost were strictly so much per unit of output up to the physical limit of capacity (which gives a reverse L-shape to the average prime cost curve) this curve would start at G, and it would be a straight line (the angle at G representing average prime cost per unit of output) coming to an abrupt corner at capacity, where it rises vertically. But we have postulated that average prime cost falls with output up to the designed capacity of the plant and thereafter rises. Over the lower part of our curve, therefore, average prime cost falls as the total rises and the angle at G grows greater. It passes through a point (at the normal capacity output) at which the straight line from G is a tangent to the curve. Beyond this point the curve grows steeper as it rises, until it becomes vertical at the output which is the absolute physical limit of capacity.

(Alternatively, the prime cost curve may be drawn in relation to the origin. The total cost curve is then parallel to it at a distance OG above it at every point.)

Mark the point N on the output axis so that ON represents normal capacity output. Let the perpendicular at N cut the total cost line in P_n.

NP_n is then the normal cost for the normal output, as conceived by the firm. If it were possible to sell (regularly, week by week) an output ON for proceeds NP_n, the firm would be covering what it regards as its full cost of production (calculated on the length of life of plant that it expects) and earning profits at what it regards as the normal rate. Draw the price line, OP_n. Then the slope, NP_n/ON, represents the price that yields these normal proceeds. This is the price which justifies the costs that are being incurred. The price which yields normal profits when normal capacity output is being sold (P_n/ON in the diagram) may be called the *subjective-normal price* for the output of the plant in question. There are elements of estimation, as we have seen, in the calculation of total costs (including selling costs), in the view which the firm takes of the profit to be made and in the determination of the normal rate of output for the plant. Subjective normal price must be accepted, therefore, as a vague concept, which may vary from one firm to another in similar circumstances.

7. EXPECTED PROCEEDS

One of the choices that is open to a firm is to change the price at which it offers its products. It cannot know

precisely what the effect of a price change would be
and our analysis must be conducted in terms of its
expectations, not of what turns out in the event.

Figure 23—continued

In the last diagram, mark OM, the rate of output
actually being sold (M may lie to the right or left of
N). MP represents proceeds at the ruling price
(NP_n/ON). Imagine the price line to swing round,
and at each price mark the point corresponding to
sales that the firm could expect to make at that
price (without altering sales pressure). In general,
as price rises above the level actually ruling, expected
sales fall below the present level, OM, and as the
price falls expected sales rise. We have now traced
out an *expected proceeds curve* showing what the
firm believes that its total receipts would be, in the
prevailing conditions, at various prices, if nothing
was altered except the price. (This corresponds
to the average revenue curve in the traditional
diagram.) It rises from the origin, for there is some
price at which sales would be expected to be zero,
passes through P, and somewhere beyond it falls to
cut the x axis, for there is a maximum quantity that
would be taken as a gift.

When the firm finds that it can sell its normal output
at subjective-normal prices (OM in the diagram is not
less than ON) it may well leave well alone, even if
expected proceeds make some other price appear more
profitable. But when proceeds are below normal it will
have to react in one way or another.

The situation where, at a price equal to subjective-
normal costs, normal capacity output is being sold,
corresponds to the conditions of a golden age. For the
economy as a whole the concept of a golden age

provided us with a basis for classifying various types of vicissitudes which an uncontrolled capitalist economy may meet in the course of development. Similarly this 'normal' position provides a base which enables us to describe the various situations in which a firm may find itself. As in the analysis of the economy as a whole, this is only a device for setting out the exercises. In reality vicissitudes follow each other continuously and there is no reason to expect a 'normal' position to be at all common.

In the following exercises we shall consider the reaction of a firm when it finds itself in unfavourable or favourable market conditions (§§8 and 9) starting from a position where costs are given. Then (§10) we consider reactions to changes in costs, market conditions being taken as given.

8 A BUYER'S MARKET

Let us illustrate a situation in which price for the moment is at the subjective-normal level for a plant controlled by a particular firm, but sales are less than capacity output. This might come about because demand for the products of the industry to which the firm belongs has recently fallen (whether as part of a general slump or from circumstances peculiar to that industry) or because capacity has been growing faster than demand, so that each firm finds itself subject to stronger competition than was ruling earlier. Or it may affect one firm for some reason peculiar to itself.

Figure 23—continued

With the same diagram, depict a situation where the subjective normal price, NP_n/ON, is being charged but less than normal capacity output is being sold. Let OM be the rate of output, M lying to the left of N.

(i) *Cutting costs*. The firm finding itself in this situation may set about trying to lower its costs. The ideal firm of the text books is always producing its output at minimum costs in any case but in reality there is no very strong pressure to keep costs down (or even to find out what they are) so long as proceeds exceed them by a comfortable margin.

The endeavour to reduce costs may take the form of genuine improvements in efficiency; of reductions in the quality of the product, which it is hoped that customers will not notice; or, where the whole industry is affected, of pressure to cut wage rates. (In a generally inflationary situation, to resist a rise of money-wage rates is equivalent to a cut when wages in general are constant.)

(ii) *Altering prices*. Would the firm be well advised to change the price at which it offers the products of the plant? To answer this question we must inquire what is believed about the effects of possible price changes in the situation that has arisen.

(*a*) *Sticky prices*. The firm may believe that both a rise and a fall in price would reduce proceeds—a rise because it would lose customers to rival firms who would not raise their prices, and a fall because other firms would not allow it to take customers from them. (This is the situation often described by a 'kinked demand curve'.)

Figure 23—continued

In our diagram, in such a case, the proceeds curve rises to a peak at *P*, which represents the highest proceeds obtainable at any price. To the left of *P* the fall in expected sales is more than proportional to the rise in price (demand from the point of view of the firm is elastic) and to the right the rise in expected sales is less than proportional to the fall in price (demand is inelastic).

In such a case the firm can do no better than leave price unchanged.

Here pure individualistic self-interest prevents the firm from cutting prices. It may also be influenced by a feeling that prices *ought* to rule at the subjective-normal level and that price cutting is a dangerous and undesirable form of competition which it would be wrong to introduce into a well-behaved industry. Finally, it may be bound by an agreement with its competitors which forbids price cutting or penalises sales above an agreed quota.

(*b*) *Price cutting*. The situation may be such that the firm believes that a cut in price would increase proceeds (demand from its point of view is elastic to a fall in price) and that the increase would be at least sufficient to cover the increase in prime costs entailed by extra output (marginal revenue would exceed marginal cost). It cannot hope to achieve subjective-normal proceeds, but it may believe that, at a lower price, the deficiency would be reduced. (This is shown in a diagram by the expected-proceeds curve rising to right beyond P more steeply than the total cost curve, so that the vertical distance between them is narrower for outputs beyond OM.)

If the firm is not prohibited by an agreement and has no inhibitions due to solidarity with the rest of the industry and no fear of difficulty in raising prices again if occasion requires it in the future, it then cuts prices. It does not, of course, follow that the expected benefit is in fact enjoyed by the firm.

Price cutting may be initiated by a firm in a strong position in the hope that rivals in a weak financial position may be wiped out so that the aggressor will be left in command of the situation when demand recovers. Contrariwise, price cutting may be started by firms in a very weak position, in a last desperate effort to snatch some sales and fend off collapse. Or it may be started by one firm merely out of fear that someone else will start it first. (After a period of price cutting an agreement may be formed to prevent it going further and to eliminate it in future.)

(c) *Raising price.* Sticky prices are common, and price cutting is also frequent. More rarely it may happen that a firm reacts to a fall in demand by raising prices. It may believe that its customers are so firmly attached that it could raise prices without suffering a proportionate loss of sales (demand is inelastic to a rise in price), so that total receipts would be higher at a higher price. (This is shown in the diagram by the proceeds curve rising to left of P.) In the past it has charged no more than its subjective-normal price, in spite of the fact that a higher price would have increased profits (though it may have fattened up its estimates of costs and of the 'reasonable' level of profits above what they would have been in a more competitive situation). Now, finding that subjective-normal price is yielding a rate of sales that fails to cover 'full costs', the firm may raise prices. (Once more, its diagnosis may have been mistaken, so that in fact it does no better than before.) It is only in these very special circumstances that the businessman's doctrine that prices are determined by costs can be literally applied in the situation of a buyer's market.

(iii) *Altering selling pressure*. An increase in outlay on advertisement and other forms of sales pressure is in some ways equivalent to cutting prices and a reduction to raising prices, but there are important differences between the two. The aggressive firm who hopes to take advantage of the buyer's market to ruin its rivals may use sales pressure as an adjunct or an alternative to price cutting, but the weak seller for obvious reasons cannot resort to it.

To some extent, advertising outlay is regarded by firms as a form of investment which they curtail when times are bad. A rise of price, as a reaction to the situation of a buyer's market, is to be expected only in peculiar circumstances, but a reduction in selling costs may be quite common.

(iv) *Multidimensional problems*. Changes in quality, price and selling costs are all interconnected in their effect on demand. For instance, a cut in price is more likely to increase sales if it is accompanied by appropriate advertising. The firm has to decide the combination of policies to be pursued quickly, without time for experimental trial and error or elaborate investigations. It can never really know what combination is the most effective and decisions must be taken largely on hunch or on some kind of conventional lore. The great variety of circumstances that firms meet with, and the great variety of policies possible in any one set of circumstances, make it impossible to formulate any simple generalisation about what will happen.

9. A SELLER'S MARKET

Now consider a situation in which sales at subjective-normal prices exceed normal capacity output for the plant that we are considering. (This is shown in the diagram by M lying to right of N.) Here proceeds exceed the subjective-normal rate (MP is greater NP_n.) For the time being the firm is making profits which are greater than it had reckoned on in setting up the plant.

(i) *Marginal cost.* At some point beyond normal capacity output, prime cost per unit of output begins to rise sharply. Let us take a case where the output that can readily be sold at the subjective-normal price lies in this region of high marginal costs, but short of the point of maximum physical capacity. It may be that at this point marginal cost exceeds marginal revenue, in the sense that if the firm refused some sales and produced a correspondingly smaller quantity of output its total profits would be greater. (This is shown in the diagram by the slope of the proceeds line being less, at output OM, than that of the total cost curve, so that to the left of P the gap between them, which represents the excess of actual proceeds over subjective-normal costs, is greater than at P.)

How should the firm react to this situation? It may well feel that it would be unwise to refuse orders merely to save marginal cost and squeeze a little extra profit out of an already profitable situation. Should the price at which output is offered be raised? The position may be such that it would be profitable, from the immediate short-run point of view, to do so, but it is not likely to be worth the trouble and the risk of damaging goodwill. The most usual policy is to continue to sell at subjective-normal prices despite the temporary excess of marginal cost over marginal revenue. In this situation there is a sense in which the businessman's doctrine, that prices are governed by normal costs, may be said to be correct.

(ii) *Excess demand.* Now consider a situation in which the output that could readily be sold at the subjective-normal price exceeds what it is physically possible to produce from the plant. If the firm either is in a monopolistic position, or believes that rival sellers are in the same position as itself, it can safely raise prices to choke back demand and make handsome profits for the time being. Alternatively, it may leave prices unchanged and ration customers and lengthen delivery dates, eking out supplies as it sees fit. In either case it is now in a vulnerable position, for excess demand, whether expressed in super-normal prices or in short-ages, is an invitation to fresh investment, and when new supplies come in, not only is the immediate seller's market killed off, but for a long future the hope of scarcity recurring is lessened and the fear of excess capacity are increased.

The best remedy against the intrusion of new rivals into a fat market is for the firm itself to enlarge capacity as fast as possible.

(iii) *'Maximising profits'.* Once more, all decisions have to be taken on inadequate knowledge of consequences, and the policies of firms may be very various in similar circumstances. In the text-book static equilibrium analysis everything is covered by the assumption that the firm has already got into a position such that nothing that it can now do will increase its profits. But in the hurly-burly of uncertain life to say that firms attempt to 'maximise profits' does not provide an adequate guide to how they behave. The most general rule (though subject to exceptions) is that the aim of firms is to survive and (with further exceptions) to grow. The important feature of a seller's market is that it is a situation in which survival is less difficult for weak firms and growth easier for strong ones. But there are a number of ways of taking advantage of it, and once more, we cannot provide any simple generalisation that will fit all cases.

10. CHANGING COSTS

Costs of production from the point of view of a firm are never constant for long. Prime costs alter with prices of materials, wage rates alter, new techniques are installed.

The reaction of a firm to a rise in costs, like its reaction to a change in demand, depends very much upon its view of how its rivals will behave. Even if all have been hit by the same change—say, a rise in wage rates—there may be some among them who prefer not to raise prices, and if so, demand from any one firms's point of view is still highly elastic to a rise in price. It must then grin and bear it, 'absorbing', as the phrase is, the rise of costs in lower profit margins. A sufficiently large rise in costs must, however, bring a rise in prices, for the smaller the remaining margin the less reluctant is a firm to lose sales and the less keen are rivals to acquire them, so that the stickiness of prices sooner or later gives way and margins are restored.

There is no such necessity for a fall in costs to lower prices. So long as no firm cuts there is no reason why any should. But with lower costs and the old price ruling, margins are higher and sales more profitable. Competition in selling may become keener, and the fall in production costs is then made up by a rise in advertisement and other kinds of selling costs.

The reaction of prices to costs is thus rather likely to be on the principle of 'Heads I win and tails you lose'. The consequent upward drift in margins, however, may be interrupted from time to time by an outbreak of price competition, whether coming from within the existing industry or as a result of fresh competition.

II. THE CHOICE OF PRODUCTS

To simplify the argument (which remains, even so, sufficiently complicated) we have been discussing price policy from the point of view of a firm which has already decided what to produce from a particular plant, but in fact the choice of products is continually coming up for revision. A firm may have only a certain range of products that it understands and for which it has market connections, but even so, there is scope for choice within the range.

The actual selection of commodities being produced from a plant at any moment is the result of decisions made in the past, some of which are proving more successful than others; and to make the most profitable use of a plant the firm must from time to time eliminate the less successful products and expand others or add new ones to its list.

To know what are the most profitable commodities to produce, the firm would have to know what are the future prospects of each, what are the relations between them—whether offering one increases or reduces the ease of selling others—and what the effect upon total costs of each possible combination of proportions of products would be. This would be an impossibly complex calculation even if all the data were available, and most of the data available are mere guess-work. The firm, here again, has to decide either on hunch or on some kind of formula.

Various conventional methods are in use for allocating costs between commodities produced, in proportion to prime cost, in proportion to floor-space occupied, or what you will, and on this basis a subjective-normal cost for each is arrived at. The price at which a particular commodity should be offered may be dictated to the firm (within narrow limits) by the prices ruling in the market for similar goods. Where it is free to choose, it must set the price (again largely on hunch) that appears most eligible, taking into account the long-run as well as the immediate effects to be expected on sales.

Commodities for which the price is less than the conventional subjective-normal cost are then rejected, and those for which price covers subjective-normal costs are regarded as profitable.

Procedure on these lines may be merely a short-cut to taking decisions which it would be impossibly complicated to work out in full. But if the firms really believe that the relation of prices to subjective-normal cost is the criterion of profitability, they may be led into serious error. When the alternative to producing a particular batch of output would be to produce something else (capacity being limited relatively to demand) which would yield a larger excess of proceeds over costs, the fact that for this particular product price exceeds subjective-normal cost does not mean that the business is worth while. On the other hand, when the alternative is to leave capacity idle, the fact that the price is less than subjective-normal cost does not necessarily mean that the business is unprofitable; a large part of the costs that have been allocated to the commodity in question have to be undertaken anyway; by not producing the commodity, only its prime costs can be saved, and if total receipts cover total prime cost they are better than no receipts.

Presumably the most successful firms are those who do not take the conventions of cost accounting too seriously.

12. INVESTMENT

The situation which we first considered (§6) in which a plant is producing capacity output and selling it at subjective-normal prices, was the result of correct anticipation by the firm that set it up. There is no reason to expect such cases to be common in reality. Investment decisions, even more than decisions about price and sales policy, must be taken largely on hunch or by convention.

The fortunate situation for a firm is to find that it has underestimated the market, so that sales are greater than capacity at the subjective-normal price or prices can be set above the subjective-normal level originally calculated. The unfortunate situation for the firm is to have excess capacity on its hands.

This consideration is analogous to that which we met with in the exchange economy—producers benefit from the scarcity of what they produce relatively to the demand for it.

On the other hand, as we have seen (§9(ii)) too great an excess of demand relatively to capacity is a danger, for it is an invitation to others to invest to supply the market.

Tension between fear of excess capacity and fear of losing markets is what governs investment plans, rather than any exact calculation of costs, prices and prospective profits.

It was for this reason that in Part Two we preferred to treat the over-all rate of net investment in a capitalist economy (freely operating without guidance from government) as something which emerges unconsciously from the competitive process rather than as a calculated response to the prospect of profit for the typical firm.

PART FIVE

A RATIONAL PRICE SYSTEM

A LARGE part of economic teaching consists of setting up an idealised image of a free private-enterprise market economy, working in conditions of perfect competition, and then throwing various bricks at it by way of exceptions and objections. The structure is now so battered that it is easier to make a fresh start and transfer the image to an idealised planned economy.

The exercises concerned with prices in conditions of perfect competition are well known and will not be repeated. In a discussion of this kind it is impossible to avoid an element of personal judgment; the argument is set out dogmatically and is intended to serve as a basis for disputation.

I. THE ROLE OF PRICES

We consider an isolated economy, free from international complications, in which production is carried on in the interests of the consumers.

The public can express their wishes to some extent individually, each family selecting from what is offered to them the things that they prefer to consume, but there are a number of decisions that can be taken only collectively and there must be political organs to decide the issues that arise in those spheres.

The division of activity between providing for present consumption and accumulation for the future has to be considered from the point of view of an immortal society, and must be taken collectively (this was discussed in Part One §12). There are some services which, for various reasons, are provided without individual payment: roads, because it is a great nuisance to collect tolls; health services and aids for the disabled, because it is considered unfair that individual families should suffer a loss of purchasing power for normal consumption on top of the drawback of having to cope with illness; education, because it is felt to be a concern of society rather than of individual parents.

The funds required to pay those engaged in investment, in the general administration and in free or subsidised services, are raised, in the kind of economy which prevails in modern democratic capitalist countries, partly under the control of individual firms, from profits (made out of the sale of goods to the public) which are set aside to finance investment and partly from funds borrowed from private savings, which also largely come from profits; partly under the control of individual income earners or property-owning foundations, from charitable donations; and partly under the control of various government agencies, from taxes assessed on income, from taxes that enter into the selling prices of commodities and from taxes on profits, which in turn are levied from the public in the prices of commodities.

There is no need to enlarge upon the great nuisance that taxation is to all concerned. In our Utopian economy, decisions having been taken at the political level as to what finance is required for investment, social services, etc., the sums can all be raised in the simplest manner, as a surplus of receipts over outlays in the enterprises producing saleable goods, that is, in the same manner as funds for investment are raised in a private enterprise economy through the medium of undistributed profits. The whole finance provided in this way forms a common fund and is laid out upon a common plan, instead of accruing haphazard to individual owners.

The over-all political decisions determine how much of the economy's total resources are to be used to provide goods and services for current consumption. Of these the public wants more than it is possible to provide, and they have to be rationed in some way or other. For the purpose of rationing scarce goods there is no better device than to give everyone an allowance of general purchasing power and to set prices at the level which equates supply and demand for each type of product.

In modern democratic nations there is a great discrepancy between the actual distribution of purchasing power between families and what is felt to be right, so that the income and price system is continuously being tinkered with by taxation and subsidies. In our ideal economy we may suppose that the distribution of money income (through earnings from different kinds of work, pensions, etc.) is generally felt to be fair.

'Fair' is not usually felt to be the same thing as 'equal'. Dangerous, unpleasant and responsible work, or that requiring long training, may 'fairly' be rewarded at more than the average rate. Whether innate talents should be rewarded is a deep question. Certainly the public delight to honour their favourites; the luxury enjoyed by film stars excites satisfaction, not envy. When the total output of the basic means of subsistence is small it is necessary to safeguard the standard of life of the lowest-income receivers and arrange matters so that super-average rewards are taken in the form of luxuries. We will postulate, however, that our Utopia has passed that stage and that the lowest incomes are not felt to be intolerably low. The distribution of money income corresponds to the distribution of real income that, by and large, is felt to be right. The price system then comes into its own as the best and simplest manner of distributing saleable goods amongst the population.

Indeed, some goods which are free, or subsidised for the poorer consumers, in welfare-state capitalism might better be included in the market-price sector in an egalitarian society. On the whole, however, the line should be shifted the other way, for under capitalism there is a strong bias in favour of leaving as large a field as possible free for private money-making. (It is only recently and only in a few countries that a free health service has been inaugurated.) The reader is invited to consider what goods and services would be included in the market sector of his own ideal Utopia.

No price system can be perfectly fair, for as we have seen (Part Three §5(ii)), when tastes and needs differ the purchasing power of money, at any given set of prices, is different for different individuals, and any pattern of prices is bound to be more advantageous to some than to others; even when money income is distributed in a manner which is accepted as equitable, the distribution of real purchasing power inevitably remains somewhat arbitrary. But this is a small drawback compared to the enormous advantages of the market system for distributing goods according to the needs and fancies of individuals.

First of all, when official prices are such as to cut back demand to equality with supply there is no scope for black-marketing except outright theft. The system polices itself and requires no administrative machinery to keep it in order. This, indeed, is the strongest argument for using prices as a regulator of demand.

For the authorities to come between a willing buyer and a willing seller is difficult, creates unpleasantness and sets up a state of hostility between the public and the administration which has far-reaching ill effects. To check theft (say by workers from factories) is much easier if other kinds of economic crime, which the public sympathises with, do not exist. The supply-and-demand pricing system is thus a bulwark of freedom and public morality.

Its second important advantage is that it allocates scarce goods to those who are most keen to have them and so (errors and omissions excepted) to those who are most likely to get satisfaction from them. Thirdly, it appears fair and reasonable that each family should pay for what it chooses to take from the common pool at the valuation that the market has put upon it.

Finally, the pricing system operates as a useful indication of the relative scarcity of various kinds of commodities and so of the directions in which it is most useful to steer existing resources that have alternative possible uses and to expand productive capacity for the future.

(These advantages of 'rationing by the purse' are of course dependent upon the distribution of purchasing power between families being regulated in a manner which is accepted as fair and reasonable.)

In the fanciful picture described in Part Three §12 we saw an ideal price system operating in extremely simple conditions. The market sector of our Utopia claims to approach that ideal as closely as is possible in the far more complicated conditions in which it has to operate.

In spite of the great advantages of regulating demand through prices, there are some circumstances in which other forms of rationing are to be preferred. For instance, if there were a reduction in the supply of some important commodity, the demand price would shoot up. More purchasing power than before would be absorbed by this commodity (the demand being inelastic) and the prices of other commodities would have to be sharply reduced to prevent unsold stocks accumulating. If the shortage is expected to be temporary, it would be better to avoid this upheaval and ration the scarce goods. When there is a housing shortage, some other system of allocation may be preferred to the market mechanism. When motor cars are scarce, they may be allocated according to usefulness to society—for instance doctors being given preference. And so forth. There is no need to stick to the market mechanism against common sense, but in our Utopian economy, commonsense indications against it would be much less frequent than they are in a society in which the distribution of purchasing power is very unequal and is not in accordance with accepted principles of social justice.

2. ORGANISATION OF THE MARKET SECTOR

In our Utopian economy production is directed by the interests of consumers, and the consumer interest cannot prevail where individual buyers confront producers. First of all, the buyer is at the disadvantage of being an amateur, while the seller is a professional; secondly individual buyers do not all react strongly to small price differences, so that sellers are not subjected to the discipline of perfect competition; thirdly there are, as we shall see in a moment, various advantages that can be won by buyers acting collectively that are inaccessible when they act individually. The consumer interest, therefore, must be organised, and the most convenient way of doing this is through the

H

agency of wholesale buyers whose business it is to negotiate with productive enterprises and fix the prices at which goods are offered to consumers.

The wholesale agents supply retailers, who are allowed a mark-up, controlled by publication of official retail prices in the shops.

Production for the market is organised in factories, farms, etc. Productive capacity has been set up as far as possible in units of the most efficient size—taking account of the available supply of managerial ability— and the business of the manager in charge of each establishment is to organise current production with the capacity that has been allotted to him. Demand is transmitted to the managers by the wholesalers at prices which correspond to demand prices in the market. Prime costs are determined by the cost of labour, materials, etc. The managers are instructed to produce in such a way as to maximise the surplus of receipts over costs. This means that, first they must endeavour to produce any given output at minimum costs; secondly they must choose the mixture of products which, at the given prices, pays them best; and thirdly the over-all rate of output must be such that they are working their plant to capacity, subject to the condition that short-period marginal cost of output does not exceed the price per unit that they receive, that is to say, they must not produce at such a high rate that a small reduction in output would reduce total costs more than receipts. The prices from the point of view of the managers are simply given, and there is nothing to be gained either by monopolistic manipulation of supplies or by special efforts of salesmanship.

A certain amount of labour has been allocated to the market sector. When it is distributed to the best advantage between different lines of production no worker could add more to the value of output if he were employed somewhere else than where he is. This means that the short-period marginal product (valued at prices that reflect consumer demand) of labour of any particular kind is everywhere equal (as we saw in Part One §18 (i)).

In the process of trying to maximise profits each enterprise seeks to equate the value of the marginal product of labour to its marginal cost from his point of view. The equality of marginal products is therefore secured if a uniform cost of labour of each type is charged to each enterprise.

It is also necessary that the over-all offer of employment by the enterprises should be equal to the available supply of labour. The profitability of employing labour for each enterprise could be regulated, without disturbing the relative prices of commodities, by charging a uniform proportional turnover tax on all sales. (In actual socialist economies the requisite over-all gap between wages and selling prices is created by turnover taxes, but they are not uniform and so introduce an arbitrary element into the relations between costs and prices.)

It is more logical and more convenient, however, to do it the other way round and to charge the enterprises a tax on their wages bill such as to raise the cost of labour to them to equality with its short-period marginal product.

When the demand for labour over all, or for a particular type, or in a particular region, falls short of supply, a subsidy to the wages bill would be required to reduce the cost of labour to equality with the value of its marginal product.

In any given short-period situation the enterprises would differ amongst themselves in profitability; some have better land or newer equipment than others; some are equipped to produce goods in greater demand. When the prices received by the enterprises are everywhere equal to their marginal costs (including the wages tax) total receipts for many will exceed total costs. These surpluses are taken from them in the form of rents charged for the productive capacity allocated to them.

Prices and costs are thus fixed so that, in struggling to make a profit, the enterprises will be guided to use the resources of the community to the best advantage to meet demand as expressed in market prices. The manager and employees of each enterprise (including the retailers) are allowed a proportion of profits to be disposed of under their own control, to give them a personal incentive to play the game according to the rules laid down.

The wholesale agents themselves are not actuated by the profit motive. They are public servants, subject to public criticism, but the finance with which they operate is provided by the state banking system, which constitutes a check upon their activities designed to prevent abuses.

The underlying principle of this system is that the resources in existence at any moment should be used to the best advantage in meeting the wants of consumers, as expressed in demand price.

Prices are regulated by demand and short-period supply. They are not fixed according to any notion of cost of production.

In the final long-run equilibrium of the text books, prices correspond to costs of production, but long-period equilibrium is never attained in real life, and there is no advantage in trying to take a short cut and impose long-run equilibrium prices in an out-of-equilibrium situation. To do so would destroy the discipline that the market imposes on producers; a cost-plus system of prices permits profits to be earned irrespective of efficiency. The proper definition of costs, as we have seen (Part Four §5) is a highly controversial matter, and, when prices go by costs, the manager of an enterprise has more to gain from efforts spent on arguing with the authorities to get some items of cost allowed than from trying to eliminate them by improved efficiency.

Above all, the pattern of prices based on costs, on whatever system costs are judged, bears no relation to the pattern of prices at which demand and supply are equated, so that there would be surplus capacity at some points and unsatisfied queues at others. The beauty of the market system would be dreadfully marred by such a wanton waste of potential output.

In our Utopia these errors are avoided. The system works in such a way as to establish as near as possible the conditions of short-period equilibrium in a perfectly competitive market, so far as current production is concerned, and while the indications of the short-run position are used as a guide in long-run planning, each short-period position, as it comes into being, has to be treated on its own merits.

Whatever pattern of prices is adopted, the financial balance of the system as a whole regulates itself. Total receipts from the wages tax and rents provide the sums required to pay for non-saleable production. When, over any period, say a year, there is net saving by the public the authorities are borrowing—whether through savings banks or additions to hoards of currency (as we saw in Part One §14). When the public is dissaving on balance, the authorities have an over-all surplus of receipts over outgoings and are reducing their debt to the public. The outgoings of the authorities are either self-balancing transactions between their own branches (as when a wholesale agency takes over a stock of goods from an enterprise) or are payments made to individuals—wages, pensions, etc. The individuals either spend what they received by buying goods and services or lend it to the government. Taking it over all, however the costs of production of goods sold to the public are reckoned, the authorities receive a surplus over costs plus loans from the public which provides for all the services in excess of those costs of production that they have to pay out.

This over-all balance maintains itself however ill or well chosen the concrete content of the stream of output that is forthcoming and however efficient or inefficient the methods of production may be. But for each individual enterprise there is a continuous struggle to avoid losses.

The foregoing is a general sketch of a system designed to offer the advantages which are claimed for a free market system and to avoid the contradictions which prevent those advantages from being realised in actual economies, both capitalist and socialist. We now proceed to examine its various features in more detail.

3. THE CHOICE OF PRODUCTS

At any particular moment the great bulk of production is dictated by already-known demands, but there is always a possibility of change in the types of commodities being produced, and, if real income is growing, new commodities must be added to the list of what is offered to the public. Our economy is run in the interests of the consumer; the choice of commodities to be produced must be made from his point of view. Certainly the managers of enterprises should be encouraged to make suggestions, for they know what is possible, but there should also be research, testing and experiment carried out by agents of the wholesale authorities, whose loyalty is to the buyer, not the seller. No advertisement by sellers is allowed, but information and critiques of commodities are available and individual shoppers are encouraged to express their wants and grievances. Due attention is paid to the durability of goods, for the aim of the wholesale agents is to get the best value for money for the consumer rather than to ensure a future demand for replacements.

How far should the design of goods be standardised? Generally speaking, standardisation makes for economies in production, so that the fewer varieties of commodities offered, the greater the bulk of stuff that can be produced with given resources.

There are some things of which it is a positive advantage to the consumer to have standardisation, quite apart from any economies in production. For instance, the dimensions of electric fittings, spare parts of all kinds of machines, anything requiring refills such as razor blades, and so forth. There are generally economies of scale also in producing such things. There is a clear indication that they should be standardised.

For another class of goods, which are purely utilitarian, the consumer is indifferent to the number of varieties offered, provided that what is offered is of a satisfactory design and in a number of sizes, etc., that correspond to real differences in function. For such goods the wholesalers should foster standardisation wherever cutting out variety increases efficiency in production.

For other things variety is an important benefit to consumers—in some cases because individual tastes and needs differ, in others (such as clothes and furniture) because an absence of uniformity is an end in itself.

All the same, for many goods it is possible to reconcile the claims of economy in production with variety in consumption. The most important economies of large-scale production are those realised within a single establishment, and, within an establishment, in having long runs of production. For most products there is a certain rate of output beyond which a further increase brings no further economies. Thus, when the total supply of a particular range of goods occupies several factories, each can produce a small range of varieties at maximum efficiency, and each be producing different varieties. Then, where transport costs are not too heavy, or the market is densely populated, there need be no conflict between the claims of efficiency and variety. Our wholesalers can place orders in such a way as to bring about the highest degree of specialisation that yields any economies and yet receive a great deal of variety.

Sometimes, however, economies of scale seem to be inexhaustible, so that however large the rate of output of a particular model of a commodity, there are still further economies that could be realised at a still larger rate of output. And often, where transport costs are heavy and sparsely populated regions have to be supplied locally, production of a number of commodities has to be carried on at less than the technically most efficient scale. In such cases, the larger the variety of production, the smaller the output per unit of labour of each particular product.

The authorities in our Utopia are in a dilemma in cases of this kind. They cannot find out what the public prefers; it is impossible to offer people a choice between a variety of models, each at a higher price, and a single model at a lower price, and then see which they prefer, for in the nature of the case each offer precludes the other. The authorities can only take a view—weighing a loss in potential physical output against a gain in satisfaction as best they may.

Our Utopia would certainly be free from the deliberate destandardisation which occurs under competitive conditions even when standardisation would be a clear advantage to the consumer.

On the other hand, our Utopian authorities could see to it that minority tastes were not neglected in the manner which is inevitable in a profit-seeking economy. There are certain commodities (say, outsize shoes, or a train between Oxford and Cambridge) which are of inestimable value to some consumers, who are not numerous enough or wealthy enough to constitute a profitable market. Here again the arbitrament of the market gives no guidance and the authorities must use their judgment.

In all this it is important to draw a sharp distinction between cases where it is essentially impossible for the needs and desires of the public to be clearly expressed through the market, and cases where the authorities decide to override market demand because it is held that the public do not know what is good for them. There may be some authority which decides that there should be, say, less hard liquor and more grand opera supplied than market demand reveals, but our wholesalers should not be actuated by such paternalistic considerations—they should be devoted to trying to satisfy the public. The fact that in some cases consumers' desires cannot be expressed purely by the market, does not mean that the authorities should impose their own views on consumers. It only means that they have to supplement the indications given in the market by other evidence to find out what the public prefers.

The whole problem of the choice of products is very sketchily dealt with in the text-book system. In real life all sorts of influences are at work extraneous to the best interests of consumers. Once more the reader is invited to consider how the matter would be dealt with in his ideal economy.

4. PRICES TO THE CONSUMER

In our Utopian scheme the wholesalers fix prices to the consumer, a margin being allowed to retailers. The influence of prices on supplies is discussed later. Here we consider the process of settling the over-all level of prices and the pattern of relative prices in such a way as to bring demand into equilibrium with available supplies.

If the over-all level of prices, in relation to the flow of money income, is set rather low, so that over-all money demand exceeds the value at those prices of the flow of output, then consumers are trying to spend more than they are able. There are frequent shortages, and queues of which the tail end gets nothing. Paradoxical as it may sound, it is far better for the consumers to have prices rather on the high side, so that the shops are full, customers inclined to be choosey and critical and retailers anxious to please— in short that there should be something of a buyer's market.

So far as relative prices are concerned, to establish the ideally correct pattern is in principle impossible when changes in income and tastes are going on; an equilibrium pattern of prices would not remain in existence long enough for trial and error to find it out. Moreover the process of carrying out experiments by altering relative prices of different commodities would itself affect the pattern of demand, for any individual who happens to buy at a high price has so much the less purchasing power for other things.

There is no need, however, to imagine that our wholesalers have to map out the entire pattern of demand at any moment. The evolution of demand and prices is continuous, and whenever we like to begin the story, some prices were already ruling. The process of getting the market into equilibrium has to be carried out by continuous adaptation from an existing situation.

For quite perishable goods prices must be allowed to fluctuate freely to clear the market from day to day, but for everything else stocks have to be carried. Prices must not be altered too frequently. When stocks of a particular commodity are running down at one point and silting up at another, the goods can be switched. When one commodity, or brand of a commodity, is proving unsaleable at the current price, while others are popular, the wholesalers see if it is possible to switch production within the existing capacity of enterprises. In so far as it proves impossible to bring supply into line with demand, and the discrepancy appears to be permanent, prices have to be altered so as to bring demand into line with supply. This is not an easy matter. As between commodities which are close substitutes from the consumer's point of view relative prices have a strong effect on demand. Thus a higher price of nylon is likely to mean a larger demand for cotton. But as between broad categories of goods, income effects are more important than substitution (see Part Three §§2 and 3). Thus, a lower price for textiles of all kinds may mean a higher demand say, for furniture or for motor cars. To predict the effects of price changes with perfect accuracy is impossible. The process of searching for equilibrium is therefore continuously going on and there is never a moment when a perfect fit has been achieved all round.

In spite of inevitable imperfections, this system is the best that can be imagined. It preserves the flexibility of the self-regulating market without either the sense-less fluctuations seen in competitive conditions (such as we discussed in Part Three §10(iii)) or the arbitrary administration of prices according to the degree of monopoly power of the seller (such as we observed in Part Four) and it operates as nearly as possible as a 'hidden hand' that regulates the economic behaviour of the public without ever giving them orders or tying them up in red-tape.

5. THE LABOUR MARKET

In our Utopian economy there are certain 'unearned' incomes such as pensions for the aged, premiums to those whom society delights to honour, and perhaps some interest on private savings, but in the main all money income is received in connection with work done, and the general principle is that income should be just about equally difficult to earn in every occupation. This involves judgment on how to weight say, the dangers of being a coal-miner against the responsibility of being a surgeon. Trades which are generally felt to be less eligible than others must carry higher hourly earnings, so that willing recruits can be found for them, and it may be necessary to pay different rates in different geographical regions. But the state of demand for the particular commodities that any group of workers happens to be producing should not affect their rates of pay. If demand for a particular commodity is expanding faster than supply, there is no reason why the workers who happen to be already in the industry concerned should receive a bonus. Or if an industry has to lose, say 10 per cent of its workers, there is no reason why the 90 per cent who are to remain should be penalised. Labour must be steered from one use to another by the offer of jobs, and the system has to operate in such a way that in each neighbourhood the number of jobs offered is equal to the number of workers available.

Each individual enterprise, loyally striving to maximise profits, wants to employ labour with its given plant, up to the point where the selling value of additional output just covers additional cost; in other words, up to the point where the addition to costs that would be entailed by employing another unit of labour would exceed the short-period marginal net product of labour, that is the value of additional product minus additional costs for power, etc.

Given its schedule of marginal net products for different numbers employed, the enterprise requires more labour the lower the cost of employing a man.

With any given pattern of prices, therefore, there is a certain demand schedule for labour, in the sense that for any given labour force there is a certain level of cost per unit of employment at which the enterprises will be willing to employ that number of men. This demand price for labour depends upon two sets of conditions. Given the pattern of prices of commodities, it tends to be higher in any particular line of production the higher the marginal physical product of labour in that line, which, in any given state of technique, depends upon the availability of the appropriate productive capacity. Thus the demand price for labour tends to be higher the better equipped the enterprises are. And, given the physical conditions, the demand price for labour depends upon the prices of the commodities being produced, and these in turn depend upon the volume of money income being spent on them and the rate of output.

With any given level of money wages ruling, the demand price for the quantity of labour available to the enterprises producing commodities for sale may exceed or fall short of the wage rate. In any given technical conditions, it is more likely to be in excess the greater the volume of incomes other than these wages and the smaller the volume of private saving—that is, the greater the volume of expenditure and the higher the level of selling prices relatively to money wage rates. (This was discussed in Part One §18(i) and illustrated by Figure 7.) Since the non-market sectors may be supposed to employ an appreciable labour force and since private saving is unimportant, we take it that an excess of the marginal product of labour over the wage is the normal state of affairs.

In order to bring demand for labour into line with the available supply, it is necessary to make the cost of employing labour to any enterprise equal to the over-all value of the marginal product of that quantity of labour to the enterprises as a whole. This is done by causing them to pay a tax at an appropriate proportional rate on the wage bill which they incur.

Each manager, striving to maximise current profits, is induced to offer employment up to the point where the value of the marginal product of labour in his enterprise is no greater than the cost of employing a unit of labour and the tax makes the cost of employing labour equal to the value of its marginal product to the system as a whole. The available labour is then distributed over the enterprises so that its marginal product is everywhere equal and the best use is being made of the available labour to supply the wants of consumers, as expressed in demand prices.

The number of jobs offered is equal to the number of workers available; since workers are anxious to find jobs, enterprises anxious to find hands and the authorities concerned to provide services to facilitate mobility, they should be able to sort themselves out so that pretty well every job is filled.

The tax can be adjusted so as to equalise demand to available supply, district by district or trade by trade (in exceptional cases it may be necessary to pay a bonus instead of charging a tax) and so the labour market can be kept continuously in equilibrium in all its parts. At the same time the system conforms to the requirement that the actual rewards for labour of various types should not be at the mercy of the vagaries of the market. They are based upon the standards of what is considered fair and reasonable in the community concerned, taking account of the views of the population as to the relative eligibility of different kinds of jobs.

6. THE MARKET FOR MATERIALS

For technical reasons various stages of production must often be in charge of separate enterprises. Sometimes the advantage of having a source of supply of a raw material under the same management as the processing of it, may outweigh technical economies of specialisation. But in many cases technical conditions dictate that the extraction and preparation of a raw material should be carried to a certain stage at one point, and the semi-manufactured material handed over to a variety of different enterprises to be used in the production of widely different commodities. On the other hand, commodities destined for a certain use can often be made from widely different materials. To get the best results from limited resources, it is necessary that the supplies of each material should be directed to the point where they contribute most to the value of output, as represented by demand prices.

To enable the market mechanism to work, there must be another layer of wholesale agencies operating between the manufacturing enterprises and the producers of materials. At any given pattern of final prices and wages costs (including the tax on the wage bill) the enterprises are asked what quantities of materials they would require at a certain price, the price first chosen being a guess at what the equilibrium value will turn out to be. Those who supply free services to the public may be given an allocation, based on some estimate of the importance of what they provide, or they may be given an allocation of money and be asked to bid with the rest. (In either case there is an arbitrary element in the allocation, but this is inevitable, for the price mechanism cannot be made to work outside the sphere where money values rule.)

The enterprises supplying materials are required to state what rate of output they can offer at the chosen price, subject to the rule that they must produce the largest quantity for which short-period marginal cost does not exceed price. Suppose that it turns out that demand for a particular material exceeds supply at the first price mentioned. A higher price is suggested by the wholesaler. This may increase the amount offered by the producers of the material. It reduces the amount required by the manufacturers who use it, and at the same time reduces the amount that the enterprises can offer (at given final prices) of the final commodities into which the material enters. These prices must be raised, which mitigates the reduction in manufacturers' requirements. When at the first price suggested it fell short of supply, the reverse process raises demand. Thus the market works out the price at which supply and demand are equated, and at this price actual transactions take place.

The process of finding equilibrium, however, is excessively complicated (as we saw in Part Three §6(iv)) for each price affects other demands. The ideal equilibrium of a perfectly competitive market can never in fact obtain exactly, and meanwhile transactions are going on at non-equilibrium prices, for production has to be carried on all the while. The lack of equilibrium shows itself in stocks silting up or running down, and this provides a signal for correction of the prices. The stocks carried must be sufficient to make frequent price changes unnecessary and deliveries must always be made at the prices agreed upon, so that the calculations of the enterprises will not be thrown out of gear. When it is found necessary to alter prices, the new prices are settled for the next round of deliveries. Thus the guidance of a competitive market can be followed without suffering its instability, and with experience, we may suppose, conditions of near-enough equilibrium come to be established.

7. PUBLIC UTILITIES AND MONOPOLIES

There are some cases in which the principle of producing up to the point where short-period marginal cost is equal to price cannot be applied. Services such as transport, domestic electricity, etc., are on tap all the time for the public to use when they like, and between one time of day and another utilisation may vary enormously. At off-peak periods marginal cost may be next to nothing. Moreover in a growing economy it is obviously sensible to lay down installations at the start to meet future demand, and meanwhile there will be excess capacity even at the peaks. This will be true also of some specialised plant in the manufacturing industries in which a single installation provides all that is required for a whole industry and in sparse markets where goods that are perishable or costly to transport are supplied from a single plant for a particular district. Here the principles of perfectly competitive markets will not help us, for in such cases there can be only a single source of supply at each geographical point, so that monopoly is inevitable and 'the competitive price' has no meaning.

(i) *Utilities.* For some services it is worthwhile to charge differential prices in order to steer demand to off-peak periods. But even at a flat rate an appreciable cost is involved in collecting payment (ticket collectors, gas meters) and there are economies in setting a price which does not vary even with the amount consumed (water is unmetered in England and electricity in Norway; in many cities there is a one-price ticket on the underground), let alone with the time at which it is taken. Moreover it would be considered unfair for the peak-load user who has no option to be charged a higher price for a worse (because crowded) service. It is by no means easy to see what is the best system of pricing for these services. To charge a lump sum for any use of the service (like a water rate) and leave consumers free to take as much as they please overstimulates demand, and is feasible only when prime costs are very low. On the other hand, when the service is charged for per unit consumed (and the charge has to be a single one because variations are difficult or expensive to arrange, or are felt to be unfair to those who are peak users from necessity), the level of charges is more or less arbitrary.

The question then arises whether the aim should be to set a level of prices that yields no more than is sufficient to cover the prime costs of running the service and so leaves the overhead to be provided as part of the free social services.

The argument in favour of this policy is that demand would be choked off by higher prices, and it is clearly wasteful for capacity to go unused when there is a demand for the service at a price which covers prime costs. (It is obviously undesirable that buses should be half empty while weary pedestrians cannot afford the fare.) On the other hand, any increase in free services means that a larger surplus has to be covered from the sales of things in general, and there does not seem to be much sense in making the public pay higher prices for everything else in order to make a particular service cheaper.

In some cases a partial solution of the dilemma can be found in a two-part tariff of some kind, by which users of the service are required to pay a lump-sum contribution to its general costs and then are supplied at a price per unit calculated to cover prime cost only. When this is not practicable, the authorities have to take some more or less arbitrary decision as to the rates that are to be charged.

Even so, they must avoid the cost-plus principle, which destroys profitability as a criterion of efficiency. Charges having been fixed, the managers concerned must be instructed, like the rest, to maximise the profits of their concerns.

(ii) *Retailers*. Retail shops, though not usually regarded as a public utility, have much in common with such services. Their 'rate of output' is not under their own control; they must be available at stated times for the public to use as they please. There is the same phenomenon of peak and off-peak periods, and the same impossibility of establishing the marginal cost of any particular flow of transactions. The simplest way of dealing with them is to permit a certain mark-up on wholesale prices, calculated for establishments of various kinds so as to cover their reasonable costs, and giving them an incentive to maximise profits so that they have a motive to be obliging and attract customers. This, in one sense, resembles the system of 'resale price maintenance', but there is a radical difference in that the level of margins is set by an independent authority representing the consumer interest and is set as a maximum, not a minimum.

(iii) *Transport.* The margin between prices at the factory door and in the shops also has to cover costs of transport, on whatever principle the latter are being charged. To follow the strict canons of the perfectly competitive system, prices at each point should vary according to the transport costs involved. On the other hand there are some advantages in the principle of 'postalisation'—the principle according to which the stamp on a letter to John of Groat's posted at Land's End is no more than one addressed to the next street. For one thing, the cost of collecting money from the public is much reduced by charging simple uniform prices. Further, it helps to equalise the cost of living in different geographical areas. From one point of view, to meet the requirements of families living in remote and sparsely populated regions is a greater burden on the resources of the economy, per unit of service provided, than to supply those in dense markets, so that it might be argued that they should pay more for what they consume. On the other hand, those families may be conferring a benefit on the rest of the community by reducing overcrowding, and they may be performing some vital service which requires them to live where they do, so that it would be undesirable to penalise them by making them pay more for the goods that they buy. The important thing is that those in charge of transport should have an incentive to minimise costs by correct routing of supplies and so forth. The manner in which their charges are fixed must be such as to promote efficiency in this sense, but the manner in which the costs are recovered from the public in the prices of goods does not really matter very much, and, within reason, a system of postalisation may be the most convenient.

The true transport costs, not the charges, must be taken into account when plans are being made for the geographical location of enterprises and distribution of population.

(iv) *Monopolies*. Where monopoly is unavoidable because a single installation has productive capacity that exceeds the total demand in the market that it can reach, the wholesalers must fix the quantities to be produced as well as the prices, so as to remove from the management the temptation to try to force up prices by restricting output. They must inform themselves of the costs involved and set prices in such a way that profits are just about as hard to earn as in the general run of enterprises, which operate according to the rules of competition.

8. PRICES TO THE PRODUCTIVE ENTERPRISES

At the moment when production for the immediate future is being planned in an enterprise, its productive capacity is given; there is a certain range of products which it is capable of turning out and with the level of wages (including tax) and of prices of materials, etc., based on those ruling at the moment the costs of various possible alternative schemes of production can be estimated. The wholesalers inform managers of the prices at which they are willing to take various commodities (on the basis of the final selling price less transport and retailing costs). Each manager selects those which he thinks his enterprise can produce at lowest cost and offers the quantities that he expects to find most profitable. The wholesalers, having thus found out the conditions of supply at one set of prices, raise their offer where the quantity falls short of their estimate of demand and lower it in the converse case, until they have achieved what they expect to give a balance. They then make out a provisional scheme of orders to be placed with the enterprises. Where, owing to an error, a manager finds himself with more orders than he can fulfil, he rejects those that he considers likely to be least profitable. If any has not enough to keep his plant working at capacity he must offer some product at less than the price which has provisionally been settled. No enterprise, however, must accept orders which do not cover prime costs (including the tax on wages) for when price is less than prime cost it is a sign that labour and materials could be made to contribute more at some other point. Where labour for some reason is very immobile, the tax may be adjusted to prevent unemployment. If orders promise to cover prime costs but do not allow a sufficient margin to cover the general overhead, including the manager's salary, the business may be subsidised and allowed to continue temporarily, but it should be reorganised or wound up as quickly as possible, unless there is some special reason (such as its contribution to developing a particular district) why it should be kept going. The process of juggling orders and prices (with any necessary reconsideration of prices in the markets for materials) having resulted in as good a fit as possible, firm orders are placed and banks are instructed to provide credits for the necessary build-up working capital. The pattern of production having been settled, it is the business of the managers to see to it that any given output is produced at minimum cost (allowing for the prevailing standard of amenities for the worker) and to be continually alert to find means of improving efficiency.

It is the business of the wholesalers to readjust orders as errors appear in their estimates, to achieve as close a fit as they may between demand and supply for each kind of output. In the ideal equilibrium that they aim at, each enterprise is being used to produce the outputs to which it is best suited, and the value of the marginal product of labour is everywhere equal, so that nothing can be gained by redistributing production amongst the enterprises; then the total productive capacity available is being used to the best possible advantage to meet the wants of consumers as expressed in market demand.

9. RENTS

At any particular moment the means of production in existence are given partly by natural resources and partly as a result of investments made in the past. The distinction between the two cannot be sharply drawn, for natural resources—agricultural land of various qualities, mineral deposits, etc.—generally cannot be used without some investment having been done—clearing, draining, opening mines, etc.; while man-made installations depend for their efficiency partly on the sites on which they stand. Nor is the distinction of any importance from the point of view of the utilisation of the resources in existence (the important distinction is between those that can and those that cannot be increased by further investment).

The means of production are grouped in the enterprises, the scale of any one type of enterprise depending partly on historical accident, partly on considerations of technical convenience and partly on the supply of managerial ability. The enterprises in general are earning a surplus over costs including the tax on wages, for capacity is being utilised fully and short-period marginal costs, which are equal to prices, in general exceed average prime cost by more than will cover general overheads.

The surpluses, however, are very different as between one enterprise and another. They vary for three sets of reasons. First, in any one line there are differences in costs due to physical differences in the means of production—variation in the soil and climate, differences in the age of machinery, convenience of sites, etc. A level of prices which only just covers costs of some producers yields a large surplus to others. For each particular line it is possible to distinguish the 'cost at the margin' (in a short period sense) that is, the average outgoings (prime cost *plus* general overhead) per unit of output in the enterprise whose costs are highest. At the ruling price for the output concerned this enterprise is achieving the lowest ratio of surplus to prime cost of any in that industry and the other producers, whose marginal cost (allowing for transport) is not less than the 'cost at the margin' of the output in question, have lower average costs and achieve larger surpluses.

Second, as between one line of production and another, the relation of prices to costs depends upon the scarcity of productive capacity of various types relatively to demand.

Finally, one enterprise differs from another in the skill of the management, in selecting the right orders to bid for, in carrying them out with technical efficiency and in generating a spirit of loyalty in the workers. The profit of the enterprise from which it is allowed to benefit should reflect only this element. Clearly it ought not to vary with the efficiency of plant or the scarcity of the particular type of productive capacity concerned; first, because it would seem unfair to those unlucky enough to be employed in high-cost enterprises; second, because it is essential to the system to use profits as a check on remediable inefficiency—differences in fortuitous circumstances should not be allowed to blunt the difference in performance of different managements; and thirdly because the instruction to managers to maximise profits has more effect the harder any profit is to earn. (So far as differences in the innate ability of managers is concerned, the best men should be set the hardest tasks and the resulting handicapping system would tend to keep them all at stretch.)

To limit profit to a reward for efficiency, the enterprises should be charged rents for their productive capacity, assessed on its surplus-earning power. It would make our Utopia altogether too Utopian to imagine the assessments of rents to be perfectly judged, but we may suppose that a fairly reasonable set of rules has been worked out, so that at least major differences are ironed out and a net profit made more or less equally difficult to earn in all establishments. Where technical efficiency unavoidably falls off with time, the rent charged to an enterprise should be made to tail off as plant ages, and it might be subject to an automatic revision based on an index of prices of the products. But, apart from these adjustments, rents should not be revised too frequently, so as to avoid penalising a growth in efficiency due to improvements within an enterprise. Their purpose is to absorb the differences between enterprises which are due to the productive capacity with which they have been endowed, and to leave them to benefit from the results of their own efforts.

These rents bear no relation to the costs that were incurred in the past in producing the means of production. They are simply a reflection of technical productivity and of scarcity relatively to demand.

10. THE MARGINAL EFFICIENCY OF INVESTMENT

The rents chargeable on plant correspond broadly to gross profits in a private enterprise economy; looking forward, the rents which it is expected to be appropriate to charge as a result of a scheme now being discussed provide the basis for a calculation of the marginal efficiency of the investment. The current level of rents in any particular line are a guide to prospective rents. Thus the pattern of prices established in any given short-period situation is a guide to investment policy.

But it cannot be followed blindly. For instance a particular commodity in short supply may be selling at a high price and so generating a high rent for the enterprises producing it, while a very small increase in supply will be sufficient to saturate demand and bring the price sharply down. In such a case there is clearly a need for some investment, but neither the high current rents nor the low future rents provide a good measure of the benefit obtained from it.

Moreover, the pattern of consumption at any one point depends very much upon supplies at other points.

If food is going to be cheaper, it may be the demand for clothes or petrol which will be increased. The resources to be devoted to public utilities cannot be judged by the surpluses (or deficiencies) in their earnings, for their charges were fixed (on whatever principle) on the basis of their costs and the amount of investment put into enlarging these services has a great effect on the pattern of demand and of costs for many other things.

An investment plan has to be mapped out as a coherent scheme, and it has to be made quite concretely in terms of particular structures to be set up at particular points. A method of planning in physical terms is likely to be simpler and more effective than one based upon calculations of marginal efficiency in money terms. When the plan has been roughed out, however, it is useful to calculate the over-all expected marginal efficiency of investment implied in it and this can be used as a check on the plan. Any individual scheme that yields much less than the over-all rate will be retained only if it can claim that it yields greater benefits than are shown in the expected money return, and individual plans that promise much more will be enlarged (if physical conditions permit) to bring a quicker saturation of demand. Within any one line of production, moreover, the method of choosing between different possible techniques on the basis of marginal efficiency is probably the best available. (This was discussed in Part One §19.)

For existing enterprises, major replacements of plant must be incorporated in the investment plan; quite minor replacements of small tools, etc., are included in prime cost. There is an intermediate range of replacements and improvements that are best left to the man on the spot and each enterprise should be credited with a part of the rents which it pays as a fund that it can draw upon at will for such purposes. (This is not to be regarded as something like the amortisation allowances of private enterprise firms, for the function of such allowances is primarily to keep financial capital intact, as we saw in Part Two §14. This conception has no place where capital is not private property.) The enterprise that cannot earn any rent enjoys no fund for replacement, and will have to be wound up, unless there are some special reasons for keeping it alive, when its plant becomes too old to permit prime costs to be covered.

II. CONSUMPTION AND THE PRICE LEVEL

As time goes by output per head is growing as a result of technical progress, accumulation of means of production, improvements in personal efficiency of management and workers and increased specialisation with the growth of total output. Various elements in increased productivity cannot be clearly separated (especially when quite new commodities are being introduced). The distinction between superior techniques and more mechanised techniques is extremely important when we are looking ahead, making an investment plan (as we saw in Part One §19). But looking back for a historical account of the changes that have occurred over the past it is extremely difficult, and (for our present purpose) not very interesting, to separate out the various elements that contribute to improved productivity.

Unless the whole benefit of increased production is to be taken out in increasing the rate of investment, reducing hours of work, and increasing free services, there will be an increase in consumption per head of saleable goods. This is brought about by reducing the over-all price level of commodities. (In the imperfectly competitive capitalist industry, the reluctance of prices to fall with costs, which we discussed in Part Four §10, means that rising money wages are necessary to secure rising real wages, but, provided that the pattern of relative money incomes has been settled satisfactorily, it is more convenient to keep money-wage rates constant, allowing a rise in purchases of saleable goods to be brought about by reducing money prices).

How are relative prices moving? The notion of a 'long-period supply curve' is not of much use to us here. Properly defined, it is a timeless concept; it purports to compare various possible equilibrium positions, with different patterns of demand, all in the same conditions of supply. (This was discussed in Part Three §7(v).) It raises a number of conceptual difficulties, but even if we knew what it meant, it would not be very interesting. It appears important only because it has been confused with the quite different concept of the path through time of the price of a commodity as the output of it is increased or reduced.

To gain some light on this question let us suppose that we compare the position in our Utopia over an interval of a few years during which the output per head of saleable goods has increased.

There is no particular reason why the authorities should have chosen to develop the various sectors of the economy in constant proportions in the manner of a golden age (such as we discussed in Part Two, II). They may have taken advantage of increasing productivity to draft more labour into the investment sector, raising the rate of accumulation, or they may have altered the ratio of free services to saleable goods. But the simplest case to discuss is that in which the labour force available to produce for the market is constant, the total of money incomes—wages, salaries and bonuses—earned in that sector are about the same at the two dates, and the volume of other incomes is also constant. Total money expenditure is then about the same as before (we assume that net private saving or dis-saving is not important). Productive capacity has increased and any index of physical output will show a rise over the period. The total sales value of the output being produced at the earlier date has fallen, releasing purchasing power to absorb the additional output. The composition of output has altered. Some commodities formerly unknown have been added, old commodities are consumed in different proportions, depending mainly upon their relative income-elasticities of demand, and many details of specifications have changed.

The total surplus per annum (in money terms) being handed over by the market sector of the economy to finance other incomes, in this case, is unchanged, but its division between wages tax and rents may have altered. The demand for labour of the enterprises may have been reduced by the investment that has taken place. For instance if an industry formerly employing labour with a low physical output per head has been mechanised so that output per head has risen sharply, while it so happens that not much more than the former rate of output is consumed, the labour released must have been found other employment and it may have been necessary to lower the wages tax so as to postpone mechanisation in other lines or to lower prices and foster demand for commodities where output per head has not much risen. (It may even have become necessary to subsidise wages.) Contrariwise, if income-elasticity of demand is high for commodities that do not lend themselves to mechanisation, the wages tax must have been raised, so as both to mitigate the increase in demand for these commodities, by causing their relative prices to rise, and to release labour to meet it by raising its cost to other enterprises. When things happen to have worked out so that an over-all fall in prices has just compensated an over-all rise in marginal physical productivity of labour, the demand price for the given labour force, and therefore the tax on wages, is the same as it was before. The over-all total of rents is therefore also the same, but since the total of productive capacity has increased the rent charged on the equipment which was in existence at the earlier date has been reduced. (This broadly corresponds to the golden-age case, in which the wage in terms of product rises in proportion to output per head and the rate of profit on capital remains constant, while the total value of capital rises in the same proportion as output. But in the golden age the increase in purchasing power required to absorb the extra output is brought about by rising money incomes, not by falling prices.)

12. PRICES IN THE LONG RUN

Taking for simplicity the over-all position in which total money outlay has not altered and the wage tax is unchanged, let us consider what may have happened to the pattern of prices, assuming that in each position conditions of short-period equilibrium have been achieved, demand and supply of each commodity being in balance. Since the composition of output has altered, we can pick out only certain commodities which are being produced with near-enough the same specifications as before. For such a commodity we can compare the old short-period position with the new one, and see how price and output have changed.

Let us draw a line round the output that was being produced in the first position and see what has happened to the prices of the corresponding output in the new position.

Taking it over all, the price level of the old output has fallen. Some inferior goods (discussed in Part Three §3) for which, with higher real consumption, there is now no demand at any price, have dropped out of production, the plant or land having been converted to other uses; or, if it were quite specific, having been scrapped and the labour transferred elsewhere. For other old commodities, still in demand, new low-cost plants have been installed, embodying technical improvements. Where output per head has risen in a greater proportion than demand at the old price, labour has been released, and prices have come down. The plant that was formerly 'at the margin' has been scrapped (for with the new prices it would not be able to cover prime costs) and any of the old plants that remain in use are yielding lower rents than before.

The labour and the purchasing power released from the lines of production where this occurs have been transferred to other old lines where income elasticity of demand was high, or to new commodities which were not produced in the first position.

But not all prices have fallen. In some cases, where limited natural resources dominate the scene and it has been impossible to increase productive capacity by investment, the supply curve for the material concerned is unchanged. The behaviour of price then depends upon what has happened to demand. The increase in total consumption that has occurred may have increased the demand for products into which the material enters. On the other hand material-saving improvements in methods of production may have occurred and substitute materials may have been developed where investment is capable of enlarging productive capacity. Sometimes a synthetic substitute for a natural material, developed in order to overcome an inelastic supply, turns out to be superior and kills off demand for the original article. Where the short-period supply curve is the same as before, price and output will be higher where demand has expanded and lower where it has contracted.

Where there has been little technical progress and an expanded demand is being met from more productive capacity like the old, prices may be the same as before or even higher (the short-period supply curve has shifted to the right and the demand curve has been raised; the new intersection may be above or below the old).

If it so happens that price is the same, the plant now at the margin, yielding the least rent or none, is like the one that was in that position before (it may not be identical, for the original one may have become inefficient with age).

Even where technical progress has been appreciable, demand for some commodities may have expanded more than output per head so that their prices have risen.

Thus it is impossible to generalise about the new pattern of prices for the old output, though we know that the over-all level of prices has fallen.

If the investment plan was well chosen and estimates have proved correct, the rents which it is appropriate to charge on the new plants that have been set up correspond to the marginal efficiency of investment foreseen in the plan. But if it turns out that mistakes have been made, they must be acknowledged. Prices must be set and rents assessed according to proper principles in the short-period situation that now exists.

If the expected prices are imposed upon the market when expectations have turned out wrong, a further loss of benefit, through misuse of existing resources, is superimposed upon the loss due to the mistaken investment.

Rents higher than those expected are a sign that demand is greater or running costs less than were foreseen, and is a sign that investment in this line should have been pushed further. Rents lower than expected may indicate a technical or managerial failure, or may show an over-investment. In each case (after any feasible short-period readjustments have been made) corrections will be introduced in the next investment plan. Thus the indications of the market are continuously used to mould supplies to fit demands.

13. CONCLUSION

Our Utopian scheme is unlike any actual price system. In the markets for primary commodities something like perfect competition rules and the concept of a short-period supply curve is not without relevance, but in our Utopia conditions are unlike those which prevail in such markets in two very important respects; the incomes of individuals are insulated from the prices of what they happen to be producing, and fluctuations in stocks prevent fluctuations in prices. In the manufacturing sector of a private-enterprise economy, competition is far from perfect, and consumers are unorganised and gullible. In both sectors the distribution of income between families is not accepted as being rational, so that market demand, as an expression of consumers' needs, is vitiated at the root.

On the other hand in the socialist economies methods of direct control have hitherto been used, rather than any market mechanism, and there is a deep-rooted objection to concepts, such as rent and marginal cost, drawn from the apologetics of capitalism. It is only just beginning to be realised that a pricing system based on supply and demand, though a bad master, may be a useful servant.

It might be maintained, indeed, that our Utopia is based on a contradiction, because a rational economic system, a conscious fitting of means to ends, is quite alien to human nature, and no system will run at all that does not appeal to pride, the love of money for its own sake or national glory.

The study of our Utopia is not intended to explain actual economic systems, nor even to provide a unique standard for judging them. It is intended only to help each reader to find out what his own standard of judgment is.

INDEX OF TERMS

Formal definitions are not in general provided, but the use of the terms listed can be seen in passages referred to.

PRINTED IN GREAT BRITAIN BY
ROBERT MACLEHOSE AND CO. LTD
THE UNIVERSITY PRESS, GLASGOW